Writing

in the Dark:

An Astronomy Stylebook

Woodrow W. Grizzle III

ISBN-10: 1492759678
ISBN-13: 978-1492759676

DEDICATION

For Professor Meyer, Grammar Queen of U.Va., whose strict instruction and attention to detail inspired me to become a better writer.

Also for Professor Lendon, whose passion for antiquity ignited within me an undying love for the Ancient Greeks, their history and culture.

CONTENTS

ACKNOWLEDGMENTS

I would like to acknowledge several people who made this book possible. First, I would like to thank my loving parents for raising me and for proofreading and critiquing this book. Thanks goes out, as well, to Robin Byrne and Adam Thanz for their work in proofreading and for their feedback during the book's development.

I must also recognize the folks in the village of Waterlily on Church Island in North Carolina, where I live. My neighbors and friends there are a tremendous source of support, and I could not have completed this work without them.

Finally, I want to thank the fine people I work with in the planetarium field, the wonderful folks in SEPA and around the world - you know who you are - those who have offered me guidance, opportunity and friendship throughout my career. Thank you all. I hope you enjoy this book and get a lot of good use out of it.

Woodrow W. Grizzle III

Church Island, North Carolina 2013

PREFACE

There is a great deal of confusion and controversy about proper usage and orthography in astronomical texts. Such difficulty arises because there are so many common and scientific names for objects: often with both being identical, except for capitalization (*e.g.* sun and Sun). I have spent many years of my life as a writer and planetarian, and, during the course of those years, I have debated correct usage with colleagues of all tenures and literary skill. Often, we either came to a consensus or stopped arguing and moved forward, but still other times, both parties left the debate with nary an inkling as to how to best proceed.

The most recent edition of the IAU style manual is from 1989. Given the extent of change to the discipline of astronomy since that time, revisions are necessary. I mean not to replace the IAU document, but to add a clear, American English-specific set of rules, which is based upon precedent, the IAU style manual, and guidelines set forth by other stylebooks, such as those of the American Institute of Physics (AIP) and the American Chemical Society (ACS).

What follows are the conventions most acceptable and applicable in writing about astronomy topics. This manual does not, necessarily, apply to script writing, where stylistic and usage choices may be intended as an aid to performance direction, and where otherwise would be unorthodox.

What is grammar?

This may sound like an elementary question, but before you read further, ask yourself in earnest, "What is grammar?" The very word may transport you back to a hot and stuffy grade school classroom, complete with green and gray tile floor, fourteen-foot ceilings, slate chalkboards, oaken desks, and an immaculately kept English teacher with perfect diction. Perhaps your fevered vision may extend to sentence diagrams floating through your consciousness, as well. O.K., that's enough reminiscing for now. Let's return to the question at hand.

Grammar is a set of structural rules that governs the composition of words, phrases and clauses in any given natural language. Grammar includes morphology (how words are formed), syntax (how words come together to make sentences), and phonology (how word sounds are organized), which are often complimented by phonetics, semantics and pragmatics (*i.e.* deep stuff). Put simply, all the rules that you have in your head right now for using any language are the grammar for that language. Those rules were put there over time through continued exposure and use, either as a virtue of being a native speaker, or from extensive instruction (for non-natives). It is all of that, up there, in the melon: what keeps you from saying, "Me are ineloquent."

Grammar has both a spoken and a written component, but most of what folks think of when they think of rules for writing is not really grammar, rather it is something called orthography.

What is orthography?

This guide is most correctly referred to as an orthography guide. Orthography is one of those terms that does not get thrown around much outside of the realm of linguistics, so, before we go any further, let us discuss orthography's meaning and usage.

Orthography is the standard way in which a language is written. It is a set of rules for things like spelling, capitalization, punctuation, hyphenation, word breaks, and emphasis. The vast majority of modern languages are written down, and, as such, each has developed its own orthography over time. Though there are dialectical variations of most languages, a language's orthography is usually based upon its standard variety.

As orthographies are language-specific, this guide shall deal exclusively with American English. As you no doubt know, there is a high degree of variance among the many forms of English used around the world. I will leave the guides for other national varieties of English for the future.

Grammar and orthography are often confused because many guides and style manuals that sell themselves as grammars include orthographical elements, such as capitalization and punctuation rules.

This guide is designed to standardize American English orthography in astronomy writing. Its goal is to help you become a better writer by equipping you with the tools necessary to produce polished, professional work. My hope is that you enjoy using this guide for many years to come.

Woodrow W. Grizzle III

Church Island, North Carolina 2013

Chapter I:

CAPITALIZATION

The proper names of all astronomical objects are always capitalized, with three notable exceptions: the eponymous components of the Earth-Moon system and the Sun.

Earth as a planet; earth as a place

The word "earth" should be capitalized when used in reference to the planet as a whole. Confusion arises because the nouns *earth, moon,* and *sun* are all instances of specific designators: nouns that can do double duty as both common and proper nouns, depending upon their context. To see this concept in action, study the following example sentences while paying close attention to tone.

a. **Some forty centuries have passed since wooly mammoths last roamed the earth.**

b. **Wooly mammoths have been absent from Earth's biosphere for nearly 4,000 years.**

The sentences above express the same information, yet they are stylistically distinct. The first sentence has what is known as an *emic tone*, suggesting that the writer is native to Earth. The first sentence also has a sense of Earth as "the world." As a rule, *earth* should not be capitalized when it refers to our planet in the sense of it being "the world."

The second sentence has an *etic tone,* suggesting a more neutral tone than the first. The writer could be from Earth or not; the tone leaves his origin unclear or indifferent. The second sentence is stylistically preferred in academic writing due to its neutrality. However, emic language can go farther toward emotionally engaging an audience, and should therefore be considered in planetarium script writing, though never at the cost of exactitude.

As a specific designator, *earth* can be used as either a common or proper noun. There can be little or no cognitive difference in the two usages, but careful consideration nets polished style. In the following sentences, *earth* is a proper noun and their tone connotes Earth as a planet. In such cases, *Earth* should always be capitalized.

c. **Beyond the orbits of Mercury and Venus lies that of Earth.**

d. **The crescent moon hung lightly above Earth's horizon.**

Earth should not be capitalized when referring to the ground beneath our feet, soil, or whenever it is preceded by the article *the*. Also, be sure never to capitalize *earth* when used in idioms, such as "where on earth," or "move heaven and earth." The only exception is when it is found at the beginning of a sentence, per common English rules.

e. **For countless generations, people have tilled the dusty earth.**

f. **The earth is home to many species of lemur.**

g. **Earth covered the moldy shovels used to dig the passage.**

h. **Where on earth did you get that pawpaw ice cream?**

The Moon and moons

The word *moon* is a bit more tricky, as it applies to both Earth's natural satellite and to those of other planetary bodies. *Moon* should never be capitalized when referring to the natural satellites of planets apart from Earth, except for when it begins a sentence.

a. **Jupiter has many moons.**

b. **Orbiting Uranus is an interesting moon called Miranda.**

c. **Moons can come in all shapes and sizes.**

Always capitalize when using *moon* in reference to Earth's natural satellite, and when it is preceded by the article *the*.

d. **The phases of the Moon repeat every 29½ days.**

e. **Selene was the Greek personification of the Moon disk.**

This distinction is to clarify that the writer speaks of Earth's moon, as opposed to one of the many other moons of the Solar System.

The Phases of the Moon

The various phases of the Moon are not capitalized when used in context. Modifiers, such as *full, crescent, first quarter, last quarter*, or *gibbous* should never be capitalized. Note also that *moon* is not capitalized when describing the Moon's phase.

a. **There was a beautiful full moon last night.**

b. **I love seeing a thin, waning crescent moon just before sunrise.**

Consider, now, these two sentences:

c. **Altogether, there are eight phases of the Moon.**

d. **Altogether, there are eight moon phases.**

The first sentence relates the phase set to a particular body: the Moon. The second sentence simply describes the set. Note that subtle difference.

The Sun

The parent star of our planetary system, Sol, presents another capitalization debacle for some. When referring to the Sun as a light in the daytime sky, do not capitalize.

a. **The sun was in my eyes for the entire drive to St. Louis.**

b. **Many ancient cultures worshiped the sun.**

Also do not capitalize when using *sun* as a modifier for a deity.

c. **The Pythia was the oracle at Delphi in the temple of Apollo, the sun god.**

d. **Utu, son of Nanna and Ningal, was the Sumerian sun god.**

If you are referring to the Sun as an astronomical object, be sure to capitalize. Unlike with *earth,* this rule applies even when *Sun* is preceded by the article *the*.

e. **Planets, asteroids, and comets are some of the objects in orbit about the Sun.**

f. **The Sun supplies most of the energy needed for life on Earth.**

Additionally, the Sun's proper astronomical name, Sol, is always capitalized.

g. **It takes about 250 million years for Sol to complete one orbit of the galactic core.**

The Solar System & other planetary systems

Perhaps one of the most confusing capitalization rules arises with the term *solar system*. The root of the term *solar* is *Sol*, the proper name of our star. For that reason, you must always capitalize when referring to our home planetary system. You must also capitalize *system* because of the connotation of it being a set of objects that go together.

a. **There are eight classical planets in the Solar System.**

b. **Uranus and Neptune are, perhaps, the most enigmatic of the Solar System's planets.**

Using *solar system* in reference to any other star's planetary system is archaic and should be avoided in most cases. If such usage is unavoidable, do not capitalize.

c. **Thanks to new observing techniques, astronomers have discovered hundreds of solar systems beyond our own.**

d. **How many solar systems exist beyond ours?**

The Solar System is typically divided into two main regions, the Inner Solar System and the Outer Solar System. The Inner Solar System consists of the volume of space centered upon the Sun with radius extending outward to include the outer periphery of the main asteroid belt, a distance of approximately 4.2 AU (628.3 million kilometers). The Outer Solar System includes all the space from just past the main asteroid belt to the heliopause, the theoretical boundary where Sol's stellar wind is halted by the interstellar medium. The exact distance to the heliopause is currently estimated to be about 19 billion kilometers from Sol, based upon the location of the Voyager 1 spacecraft on September 12, 2013, when NASA scientists confirmed that it had left the Solar System and entered interstellar space. Since mid-2012, Voyager 1 had been detecting rapid increases of cosmic rays, a state hypothesized to be associated with approaching the heliopause.

Each word of *Inner Solar System* and *Outer Solar System* should always be capitalized.

e. **The terrestrial planets are all located within the Inner Solar System.**

f. **Distances between the planets of the Outer Solar System are far greater than those between the inner planets.**

The terms *heliopause, stellar wind* and *interstellar medium* are always written in lowercase, except when they begin a sentence.

g. **Stellar wind is composed of charged particles released from the upper atmosphere of a star.**

h. **The interstellar medium is made up of rarified hydrogen and helium that permeates interstellar space.**

Equinoxes & Solstices

The four points along Earth's orbit that mark the transitions between astronomical seasons are the equinoxes and solstices. Traditionally, these moments have been labeled in such a way as to be season-specific (e.g. vernal, or spring equinox). Because Earth's seasons are opposite between hemispheres, using such language can become confusing when writing for a global audience. For clarity's sake, use terms that are not season specific.

> **Northward equinox = March equinox = northern vernal/southern autumnal**
>
> **Northern solstice = June solstice = northern summer/southern winter**
>
> **Southward equinox = September equinox = northern autumnal/southern vernal**
>
> **Southern solstice = December solstice = northern winter/southern summer**

These terms are heliocentric; they deal with the Sun's position in Earth's sky over the course of the year. For example, the term *Northward equinox* means that the Sun has reached the celestial equator and its declination is continuing to increase, moving toward its maximum positive value of approximately +23.5°. Another way of thinking about it is that, because of Earth's axial tilt, after this point in Earth's orbit, the Sun will be shining continually more directly onto Earth's northern hemisphere, culminating at maximum when Earth reaches its Northern solsticial point.

Cardinal directions are not usually capitalized (unless they begin a sentence or describe a region (*e.g.* the American South), but you should always capitalize in the case of equinoxes and solstices because the directional words are proper modifiers.

a. **Summer begins in Lesotho when Earth reaches the Southern solstice.**

b. **Horseshoe crabs in the Chesapeake begin to spawn near the full moon closest to the Northward equinox.**

Should you choose to use older terms for the equinoxes and solstices, do not capitalize the season name.

c. **Orthodox Easter is observed on the first Sunday, after the first full moon, after the spring equinox, after Passover.**

d. **The summer solstice is in June for the northern hemisphere.**

If you use the month names, always capitalize, per usual English rules.

e. **The Sun's declination reaches -23.5° at the December solstice.**

f. **Hours of daylight and dark are again equal at the September equinox.**

Note that *equinox* and *solstice* are never capitalized, regardless of stylistic choice.

Cross-Quarters

Exactly halfway in between the equinoxes and solstices are the cross-quarters or cross-quarter days. Though they are somewhat less known, especially in the New World, it is, nonetheless, important to observe proper form when communicating them. Each cross-quarter has a Gaelic festival associated with it.

Lughnasadh [*LOO-nuh-sah*] **- August 1**

Samhain [*SAH-wehn*] **- November 1**

Imbolc [*IM-olk*] **- February 1**

Beltaine - May 1

Cross-quarter days and festivals are always capitalized.

   a. **Groundhog Day descends from the Gaelic festival of Imbolc.**

   b. **People dress in horrific costumes and light bonfires all over the countryside during Samhain.**

Planets

The names of the various planets in the Solar System are always capitalized.

   a. **Four planets have ring systems: Jupiter, Saturn, Uranus and Neptune.**

   b. **Do you think there ever was life on Mars?**

While the planets of our planetary system were named for mythological figures, planets outside of it are named differently. Planets that orbit stars other than Sol are called extrasolar planets, or exoplanets. The International Astronomical Union (IAU) has not agreed to a standard naming system for extrasolar planets, but there is a system in common use. Typically, extrasolar planets are cataloged by extending their parent star's proper name or designation using lowercase letters, beginning with *b* and continuing through the alphabet in order of discovery. For example, the first planet discovered in orbit about 55 Cancri is cataloged as 55 Cancri b, the second planet discovered is 55 Cancri c, and so forth. It is considered unlikely that a planetary system would ever have more planets than there are available letters.

  a. **The first confirmed extrasolar planet orbiting a main-sequence star was 51 Pegasi b.**

  b. **The third planet discovered in orbit about μ Arae is μ Arae d.**

Dwarf Planets

Dwarf planets are larger planetary objects that are neither planets nor satellites. The IAU defines a dwarf planet as an object that has sufficient mass for its shape to be controlled by gravitation (*i.e.*, a spheroid), but, unlike a planet, it has not cleared its orbital region of other objects or debris. The proper names of dwarf planets (and their moons) are always capitalized.

  a. **New Horizons was the first Earth mission to Pluto.**

  b. **The dwarf planet Haumea has two moons, Hi'iaka and Namaka.**

Asteroids

The verbal portion of the object's name is always capitalized, even when its name begins with a number.

a. **Dactyl was the first asteroid satellite discovered; it orbits 243 Ida.**

b. **Asteroid 4581 Asclepius missed Earth by only 700,000 kilometers in 1989, passing exactly where the planet was only six hours earlier.**

Please see *Naming Conventions - Asteroids (page 24)* for more on asteroid name orthography.

Comets

Please see *Naming Conventions - Comets (page 30)* for more info on comet name orthography.

Meteors

Meteors are bright streaks of light caused by meteoroids burning up due to friction upon entering Earth's atmosphere. The light mostly comes from heat energy ionizing the air around the trail of glowing particles that the object sheds as it descends. A meteoroid is defined by the IAU as "a solid object moving in interplanetary space, of a size considerably smaller than an asteroid and considerably larger than an atom." Meteors occur so often that they do not typically receive names.

Fireballs and Meteorite Falls

An exception is for notable fireballs documented as having been witnessed by many people. These fireballs may or may not have a meteorite associated with them. Fireballs without meteorites associated with them are often referred to as "events," while they are usually called "meteorite falls" when meteoritic material is found to be associated with the apparition of the fireball. There are exceptions, as there are no formal rules. These events are generally named for the place in which they occur, and they are always capitalized.

a. **The Cando Event occurred over the village of Cando, Galicia, Spain on January 08, 1994.**

b. **The Chelyabinsk Meteor was associated with an asteroid that entered Earth's atmosphere on February 15, 2013.**

Meteor Showers

Meteor showers occur when Earth passes through the debris field left behind by a (usually) cometary body when it passes through the Inner Solar System. These events are named according to their radiant point, which is the point in the sky from which the meteors appear to originate. Since our sky maps are organized by constellation regions, meteor showers are named using the constellation containing the radiant. Meteor shower names are always capitalized.

c. **One of the most prolific of meteor showers is the Leonids of November.**

d. **The Geminids and Quadrantids are the only major meteor showers not caused by a comet.**

Stars

Compared with the total number in existence, relatively few stars have proper names. These names are all proper nouns, and, as such, they should always be capitalized.

a. **Another name for δ Draconis is Aldib.**

b. **Far off in Capricorn lies the Algiedi Prima system.**

The use of genitive forms of star names, apart from that of the Sun, is rare, but these should always be capitalized. For specific extrasolar planetary systems, the star name should be used per the convention stemming from our own planetary system: Sol's system = Solar System. Thus, the planetary system about Fomalhaut, for example, is most correctly referred to as the *Fomalhaut* (or *Fomalhautian*) *System*.

c. **The first exoplanet imaged at visible wavelengths is in the Fomalhaut System.**

The following stars have both proper names and known planetary companions.

> **Errai (γ Cephei)**
>
> **Fomalhaut**
>
> **Pollux**
>
> **Rigel Kent (α Centauri)**
>
> **Sol**

Supernovae

Supernovae are stellar explosions of incredible energy. The brightness of a star becoming a supernova can briefly surpass that of its entire home galaxy. When supernovae are discovered, they are given temporary designations that are based upon the year in which they occur and the order of their discovery. The names are formulated as *SN*, followed by a space, followed by the four digit Gregorian year, followed by a letter. Uppercase alphabetical sequence *A-Z* is used first, followed by lowercase *a-z*, if necessary.

   a. **The light from SN 1987A reached Earth on February 23, 1987.**

   b. **Supernova SN 1940B was the first Type II supernova observed from Earth.**

Constellations

Always capitalize the nominative form of constellation names. When the whole name of a constellation is used, such as *Orion, the Hunter*, notice that there is always a comma after the nominative form, followed by the article *the*, and the capitalized descriptor.

   a. **There are two triangles in the sky: Triangulum, the Triangle, and Triangulum Australe, the Southern Triangle.**

   b. **One of the oldest constellations is Piscis Austrinus, the Southern Fish.**

Always capitalize the genitive form of constellation names.

    c.   A nearby Sun-like star is δ Pavonis.

    d.   Thuban, also known as α Draconis, was once Earth's northern pole star.

Deep Sky Objects

The names of deep sky objects are always capitalized. This is true whether the name is official or colloquial.

    a.   One of the first deep sky objects students learn to find is the Ring Nebula in Lyra.

    b.   They can then locate the famous Double Double.

The names and initials of object catalogs, such as Messier and New General Catalogue, are always capitalized.

    c.   In the constellation Scorpius, along the plane of the Milky Way, lie the open clusters M6 and M7.

    d.   There are many other lenticular galaxies similar to NGC 1138.

Galaxies

The names of galaxies follow the same conventions as other deep sky objects in that they are always capitalized. Always capitalize *Galaxy* when referring to our home galaxy, the Milky Way.

a. **Earth is but one of countless planets that no doubt exist within the Milky Way.**

b. **Voyagers 1 & 2 are on their way to other parts of the Galaxy.**

Other galaxy names are always capitalized, as well.

c. **The Andromeda Galaxy is the most distant object visible to the naked eye.**

d. **The Large and Small Magellanic Clouds are small galaxies that may be orbiting the Milky Way.**

Spacecraft, Rockets & Missions

The names of spacecraft, rockets and missions should always be capitalized.

a. **There have been many iterations of the Titan rocket.**

b. **The Ares rocket series were the Shuttle-Derived Launch Vehicles to be used in the now-cancelled Constellation Program.**

Different conventions apply whenever a number follows the name of a rocket, spacecraft or mission. Typically, if the number following a rocket type name is 10 or less, the number is written as a roman numeral.

c. The Saturn V was the largest rocket ever built by the Americans.

d. Between 2000 and 2005, NASA launched six Atlas III orbital launch vehicles.

Arabic numerals are usually used if a rocket designation is greater than ten.

e. The Titan 34D was a rocket used primarily for military launch operations.

Arabic numerals are also typically used if the number follows a spacecraft or mission name.

f. Pioneer 10 became the first spacecraft to achieve escape velocity from the Solar System.

g. STS-1 was the first orbital flight of the Space Shuttle Program; "STS" stands for Space Transportation System.

There are exceptions to all the above customs.

Chapter II:

NAMING CONVENTIONS

In the interest of helping writers to understand the reasoning behind the orthography related to astronomical objects, particularly small solar system bodies (SSBs), which have intricately derived titles, this section on naming conventions is here presented.

Planets

The five planets visible from Earth have been known since ancient times. Their official names are derived from the Latin versions of their ancient ones. The two planets discovered telescopically, Uranus and Neptune, were given their mythological names only after some time and controversy. William Herschel, the discoverer of Uranus in 1781, wanted to call it *Georgium Sidus* (Latin for "George's Star") in honor of George III, (then) King of Great Britain, France and Ireland. The name *Uranus* was first proposed by the German Johann Bode, who calculated its orbit, but that name did not come into official use until 1850. Similar controversy took place over the naming of Neptune upon its discovery by Johann Galle (using calculations by Urbain Le Verrier) in 1846. Names first put forward included *Le Verrier* and *Oceanus*. However, the controversy was short-lived, and acceptance of the name Neptune became fairly ubiquitous by the end of its discovery year.

Asteroids began to be discovered starting in 1801. The first asteroids were found between the orbits of Mars and Jupiter, and they were considered to be planets at first. Like planets, they were given classical names like Ceres, Pallas, and Vesta. As similar discoveries began to flood in, these minor planets were stripped of their full-fledged status. When Pluto was discovered in 1930, it was considered to be a planet because it existed in a different realm: beyond the orbit of Neptune.

In late 20th and early 21st centuries, other objects, some more massive than Pluto, were discovered beyond Neptune's orbit. These discoveries cast doubt as to whether Pluto, and other similar objects in the Outer Solar System, should be considered as planets. Such objects were usually classed as either trans-Neptunian objects (TNOs) or Kuiper belt objects (KBOs). In 2006, the IAU voted to create a new category of objects, dwarf planets, into which Pluto and similar objects would be put, to resolve the controversy. As with many things in science, the answer generated more questions, and so the controversy continues.

Natural Satellites & Rings

Newly discovered satellites and rings first receive provisional designations before they are formally named. The formula is based upon the year, the parent body and the discovery sequence. The year is simply the four-digit Gregorian year. The parent body is signified by a letter (see Fig. 1). The discovery sequence is an arabic numeral. Thus, a newly discovered object designated S/2012 U 1 would be the first new satellite of Uranus discovered in 2012. An object designated as R/2017 N 2 would be the second new ring of Neptune discovered in 2017. The *S/* stands for *satellite*, *R/* stands for *ring*. On the next page is a table showing each planet's signifying letter.

Fig. 1: Planet Letter Codes for New Satellite and Planetary Ring Discoveries

Planet	Letter
Mercury	H*
Venus	V
Earth	E
Mars	M
Jupiter	J
Saturn	S
Uranus	U
Neptune	N

"H" stands for Hermes, the Greek version of the Roman deity Mercurius (Mercury), the messenger of the gods. It is used to maintain the one-letter scheme and avoid confusion with "M" for Mars. It should also be said that it is unlikely that any new satellites of the inner planets exist to be discovered.

Asteroids

Newly discovered asteroids are named up to twice: always once with a provisional designation, and sometimes again, with a formal name, once its orbit has been established.

Provisional designations:

Provisional designation is the cataloging of objects immediately after their discovery. The provisional designation can become superseded by a permanent, or formal, name once the object's orbit has been reliably calculated. There are so many minor planets currently being discovered that most will likely never be named formally. Provisional designation can seem complex at first, but it is logical and it becomes relatively simple once the system is learned.

The system used today was first put into place in 1925. The large number of minor planets being discovered during that era made devising a new, methodical system a necessity. Since that time, the discovery rate has only increased, thanks to improvements in technology and observing methods.

The first element of the provisional name is the four-digit Gregorian discovery year, followed by two letters, which are, in turn, followed by an optional number that is sometimes written in subscript.

The first of the two letters represents the half-month in which the object's initial discovery was made. The letter *A* represents the first half of January (January 1-15), and the letter *B* represents the second half of the same month. The letters continue through the English alphabet until the end of the year, with Y being the final letter used. The first half of a month is always considered to be made up of days 1-15, regardless of the total number of days in the month. Therefore, C represents February 1-15, and D represents February 16-28 (or 29 in leap year).

The second letter indicates the object's discovery order in the given half month. So, the first object discovered in the second half of October 2010 would be provisionally designated as 2010 UA. The second object discovered during the same time period would be 2010 UB, and the letters would continue through to Z.

In modern times, objects are discovered with such frequency (due to automated search techniques) that there are occasionally not enough letters to accommodate this scheme in a given half-month. To preserve the system, a subscript number is added to indicate the number of times that the letters have been cycled. So, the twenty-seventh object discovered in the second half of October 2010 would be 2010 UB_1.

The following charts show how the letters and numbers are used in minor planet designation.

Fig. 2: Annual Half-month Letter Codes for Provisional Asteroid Naming

First Letter			
A	Jan 01	N	Jul 01
B	Jan 16	O	Jul 16
C	Feb 01	P	Aug 01
D	Feb 16	Q	Aug 16
E	Mar 01	R	Sep 01
F	Mar 16	S	Sep 16
G	Apr 01	T	Oct 01
H	Apr 16	U	Oct 16
J	May 01	V	Nov 01
K	May 16	W	Nov 16
L	Jun 01	X	Dec 01
M	Jun 16	Y	Dec 15

Fig. 3: Discovery Order Letter Codes for Provisional Asteroid Naming

Second Letter			
A	1	O	14
B	2	P	15
C	3	Q	16
D	4	R	17
E	5	S	18
F	6	T	19
G	7	U	20
H	8	V	21
J	9	W	22
K	10	X	23
L	11	Y	24
M	12	Z	25
N	13		

Fig 4:   Subscripts for Provisional Asteroid Designation

Subscript											
none	1	2	3	4	5	6	7	8	9	...	n
0	25	50	75	100	125	150	175	200	225		$25 \cdot n$

All of this information may seem overwhelming. If you feel overwhelmed, that is O.K., because the sheer number of asteroids out there is quite large, and the discoveries roll in quite quickly sometimes. To put it into perspective, a story from Earth can help clarify things. For this story, let's go back in time a few years to a small corner of North America, circa 1985.

I grew up on a farm in the mountains of Virginia. One of the things with which we were bountifully blessed was rocks: big rocks, little rocks, chert rocks, flint rocks. When you plow new ground, the first thing you need to do is remove as many rocks as possible. When I was little, one of the first jobs I had was to go out into the newly plowed fields, pick up the rocks, and put them onto a wooden sled. That sled was pulled, not by a tractor, but by a stout Clydesdale named Jim. Jim and I would spend the day driving the sled through the field, picking up rocks. When the sled became full, we would drive to the edge of the woods, where I would pitch the rocks off into a great pile. Over the years, these rock piles grew to tremendous proportions. The Appalachian countryside is full of such piles: every farm has at least one for each cultivated field. Imagine rocks ranging in size from a golf ball to a bowling ball in a pile some 10 feet high and 40 feet long, and you will have a pretty good mental picture of the scene. Imagine now giving each rock in the pile a name, and then imagine coming across another one of those piles every fifteen days, when you will repeat the process. Running out of names should not seem like a foregone conclusion.

Formal Naming

After an object receives a provisional designation, the discoverer is given an opportunity to propose a name to the IAU. Under IAU rules, the names must be pronounceable and, preferably, one word. The word is preceded by a number that reflects the sequence in which the object's orbit is precisely determined. For example, the asteroid named in honor of deceased planetarian and amateur astronomer Mike Sandras is 18434 Mikesandras. Since 1982, names are limited to sixteen characters. Letters with diacritics are acceptable, but are sometimes omitted when written, particularly in English publications. Political or military names are unacceptable, unless the person has been dead for over a century. Names that reflect capital success or advertising are never acceptable.

In recent times, there have been a number of automated object detection initiatives, such as Lincoln Near-Earth Asteroid Research (LINEAR) and Near-Earth Asteroid Tracking (NEAT). The many thousands of bodies discovered by these projects has overwhelmed the naming system, causing the IAU's Committee for Small Body Nomenclature (CSBN) to limit naming to a maximum of two names per discoverer every other month. For this reason, the majority of objects do not have formal names at this time.

More strict naming schemes apply to asteroids that belong to certain dynamic groups. Asteroids that approach or cross Earth's orbit are known as Apollo asteroids, and they are usually named for male Greek gods, heroes or other characters. Trojan asteroids, which share the orbit of a planet at Lagrangian points L4 and L5, are named for heroes of the Trojan War: L4 trojans are named for Greeks, while those at L5 are named for Trojans. Originally known to exist only in association with Jupiter, other trojan populations have been discovered in recent years that share orbits with Neptune, Uranus, Mars and Earth. Asteroids that cross or approach a giant planet's orbit, but are not in a stable resonance with it, are named for Centaurs of Greek myth. Objects in resonance with Neptune are named for characters associated with the underworld. Classical Kuiper Belt Objects (KBOs) are given names associated with creation myths from various cultures.

Comets

Newly discovered comets are named up to twice: once with a provisional designation, and then again, with a formal name once its orbit has been established.

Provisional designations

The practice for provisional comet designation is similar to that of asteroids. In the case of comets, the designation consists of the year of discovery, followed by a space, a single letter indicating the half-month of discovery within that year, and finally a number indicating the discovery sequence. Thus, the sixth comet discovered in the first half of April 2017 would be designated as 2017 G6.

If a comet breaks apart, each piece is given the same provisional designation as the parent body, with the addition of a suffixed letter. If a fragment itself breaks apart, a subscript number is added after the original fragment's letter. An example is Comet Shoemaker-Levy 9 (D/1993 F2), which impacted Jupiter in July 1994. The comet broke up into at least 21 fragments before impacting the giant planet. Nineteen fragments were designated as fragments A-W (letters I and O are not used to avoid confusion with numbers). Before final impact, fragments P and Q split in two and were labeled as fragments P1, P2, Q1 and Q2.

Sometimes an object that was once thought to be an asteroid will develop a cometary tail. When this happens, the object retains its original designation. An example of this is the case of object 1954 PC, which turned out to be Comet Faye, and so one designation of that object is 4P/1954 PC. The prefix "4P" tells us that it is a comet.

There are four possible letter prefixes for comets: P, C, D, and X.

Periodic comets receive the designation of "P." They are comets that have an orbital period of less than 200 years, or have been observed during multiple perihelion passages. Comet Halley is the most famous periodic comet. These comets receive a number as part of their prefix once a second perihelion passage has been confirmed. The numbers increase in order of confirmation, so Comet Halley is 1P/Halley because it was the first comet to be recognized as being periodic.

Comets that do not meet the criteria for being periodic receive a designation of "C." It is important to note that such comets could switch to "P" if they are later determined to be periodic.

Lost or disintegrated comets receive the designation of "D." Comet Shoemaker-Levy 9 is designated as D/1993 F2.

There are also historical comets that are known from old records, but for which a reliable orbit cannot be calculated. Such comets receive the designation of "X." The Great Comet of 1106 was such a comet. It appeared in early February 1106, and it was observed by astronomers across the northern hemisphere until mid-March of that year. Its designation is X/1106 C1.

Formal Naming

Comets are named after their discoverers. For example, the parent body of the Leonid meteor shower, Comet Tempel-Tuttle, was discovered independently by Ernst Tempel in 1865 and Horace P. Tuttle in 1866. (News traveled more slowly in those days.) The IAU prefers to credit two discoverers at most, but more are permissible in certain circumstances.

Satellites of minor planets

Provisional naming of minor planet satellites, such as asteroid moons, is the same as that of classical planets. In the case of minor planets, the planet letter code is replaced with the minor planet's designation number in parentheses.

Chapter III:

ADJECTIVALS

of

PLANETARY BODIES

This section details adjectival forms of planetary body names. When more than one adjective is given, the most commonly used form appears first. Here you will encounter three types of adjectival forms: independent adjectives, product (or origin) adjectives, and demonyms. Independent adjectives are those that are free of connotation beyond simply modifying a particular noun. Product adjectives tell us something about a noun's origins. Demonyms are a special case.

A demonym is the name for a resident of a locality. They are usually, but not always, derived from the locality's name. For example, a resident of the United States of America is known as an American, a resident of Cyprus is a Cypriot, and the common English term for people of the Netherlands is Dutch. Another word for demonym is *gentilic*. The word *demonym* comes from the Greek δῆμος (*demos*), which means "populace," and the suffix *-onym*, meaning "name." Though demonyms are well-known words, the term itself is quite obscure outside of geographical and anthropological circles. Though they traditionally describe people or other living things endemic to a given region, demonyms can be used to describe inanimate objects, as well.

Regarding pronunciation, it is important to remember that the ending *-ian* is typically unstressed, while the ending *-ean* is typically stressed.

Sol and the Planets

There are many adjectival forms for the Sun and its eight planets. Some come from their official names, while others stem from the ages of astrology and myth. This section deals with both adjectival forms and demonyms for the Sun and planets, beginning with the Sun and continuing outward to Neptune.

☉ *Sol*

Nominative	Adjectival	Demonym
Sol	Solar	Solarian
Helios	Heliacal	Helian

The Sun's Latin name is *Sol*, thus the adjectival form of this name is *solar*. The Greeks called it *Helios*, the Titan of the Sun and the personification of the Solar disk. The adjectival form of the Greek name is *Heliacal*. The Sun's symbol is the Solar disk.

☿ *Mercury*

Nominative	Adjectival	Demonym
Mercury	Mercurian Mercurial	Mercurian
Hermes	Hermean	Hermean
Cyllenius	Cyllenian Cyllenean	Cyllenian
Apollo	Apollonian	Apollonian

The planet Mercury is named for the Roman god Mercurius. He is the patron god of commerce, eloquence, travelers, luck, trickery and thieves. He is associated with quickness, and he is the guide of souls on their journey to the underworld. It is for these reasons that the ancients associated the fleetest of celestial wanderers with him.

The Greek counterpart to Mercurius is Ἑρμῆς *(Hermes)*. One of Hermes' epithets was Κυλλήνιος *(Cyllenius)*, a name derived from Κυλλήνη *(Mount Cyllene)* in Arcadia, where he had a temple. It was also upon that mountain that Μαια *(Maia)* was said to have given birth to him.

The Greeks called the planet Hermes when it appeared in the evening sky, and they imagined it as Ἀπόλλων *(Apollon* or *Apollo)* at dawn, bringing the sun across the horizon.

The planet's symbol represents the caduceus, the serpent-entwined rod borne by Hermes.

♀ *Venus*

Nominative	Adjectival	Demonym
Venus	Venerian Venerial Venusian	Venusian
Cytherea	Cytherean	Cytherian
Hesperus	Hesperian	Hesperian
Phosphor	Phosphorian	Phosphorian
Lucifer	Luciferian	Luciferian

The planet Venus is named for the Roman goddess of beauty, sex, fertility and love. Sexually transmitted diseases, traditionally known as venereal diseases, derive their name from hers.

The Greek equivalent of Venus is Ἀφροδίτη *(Aphrodite)*. Aphrodite is also known by her epithet Κυθήρεια *(Kuthêrias, Cytherea)*, which comes from Κύθηρα *(Cythera)*, home to one of her cults and her claimed birthplace.

When it appeared in the evening sky, the Greeks called it Ἕσπερος *(Hesperos)*, the Evening Star. The Roman equivalent is Vesper, which is the origin of words associated with the long hours, such as "evening," "supper," and even "west." Hesperus is the son of Eos, the dawn goddess, and the brother of Phosphorus, the Morning Star (again, the planet Venus). When the planet was spied during the day, it was sometimes called Lucifer. The planet's symbol reflects the shape of the goddess' hand mirror.

⊕ *Earth*

Nominative	Adjectival	Demonym
Earth	Earthly	Earthling
Tellus	Telluric	Tellurian
Terra	Terran Terrestrial	Terran Terrestrial
Gaea	Gaean	Gaean
Gaia	Gaian	Gaian

Earth, our home, has many names. The word "earth" comes from Middle English *erthe*. Before that, it was Old English *eorthe*, where it shares kinship with Norse *Jörð* (pronounced approximately "yearth"), who was the mother of Thor. In all cases, Earth is personified as a goddess and motherly figure.

Tellus was the Roman goddess of the earth from the early times of the REGNVM ROMANVM, or Roman Kingdom (c. 753 B.C.), through the end of the Republic. After the dawn of Empire, somewhere around 27 B.C., when Julius Cæsar's adopted son Octavian adopted the title of Augustus, Tellus and Terra Mater ("Mother Earth") became more or less indistinguishable.

The Greeks called her Γαῖα *(Gaia)*, one of the primordial deities and the mother of all. She was the Creator of the earth and all the cosmos, the Titans, Giants and gods of the heavens and of the sea. Being the mother of all things, it is fitting that the Greek word γαῖα (pronounced "GEE-uh"), meaning "earth," is of unknown origin, and is therefore a word whose root may go back to the very beginnings of human utterance. What a thought that the genesis of language may be in a call for one's mother.

An humble globe inscribed with an equator and a meridian make up our planet's symbol.

☾ *Moon*

Nominative	Adjectival	Demonym
Luna	Lunar	Lunarian
Selene	Selenian	Selenian
Cynthia	Cynthian	Cynthian

Earth's natural satellite has gone by many names over the ages. Today, we simply call it Moon, a term that has no adjectival or demonym. Instead, we use the term *Luna*, the Moon's Latin name, for that purpose. The Greeks associated two deities with the Moon. One was Σελήνη *(Selene)*, who was the personification of the Moon disk. The other was Ἄρτεμις *(Artemis)*, goddess of the hunt, who was probably associated with the Moon because of the crepuscular nature of many prey animals. One of Artemis' epithets was Κυνθία *(Cynthia)*, derived from Κύνθος *(Mount Cynthus)*, on the Isle of Delos in the Cyclades, where she had a temple. It was atop Mount Cynthus that Λητώ *(Lētó)* gave birth to Artemis and her brother Ἀπόλλων *(Apollōn/Apollo)*.

The Moon's symbol is a simple crescent.

♂ *Mars*

Nominative	Adjectival	Demonym
Mars	Martian Martial	Martian
Ares	Arean	Arean

The planet Mars is named for the Roman god of war, Mārs, or Martis. He was characteristic of Roman origins, as he was associated with both war and as a guardian of agriculture. The Greek counterpart deity is Ἄρης *(Ares)*. Though they are often put forward as equivalents, there is a fair bit of difference between Mars and Ares. Ares appears in Greek literature as a symbol of the violence and chaos of war, while the Roman Mars is the personification of how military might and generalship can be used toward constructive ends. This is in keeping with the Roman ethos of improvement through martial might: the word "martial" here being operative. In this way, Mars is more like Athena than Ares. Athena was the Greek goddess of strategy, wisdom, and civilization. She was often portrayed as a warrior of great skill and foresight, with her familiar owl always by her side. It is from this association that our modern wise old owl gets his reputation.

The shield and spear of Martis symbolize this tiny, red world.

♃ *Jupiter*

Nominative	Adjectival	Demonym
Jupiter	Jupiterian	Jupiterian
Jove	Jovial Jovian	Jovian

The planet Jupiter is named for the Roman god Iuppiter, also known as Jove. He was the chief deity in the Roman pantheon, the king of the gods, and god of the sky, lightning and thunder. His sacred animal was the eagle, which was emblazoned upon the shields and armor of Roman soldiers, and held toward the heavens atop Roman standards. The eagle flies among the stars, as well: in the constellation Aquila, which means "eagle" in Latin. The heraldic eagle flies today over the United States, the reborn Roman Republic, as it was envisioned by the Framers over two centuries ago.

The planet's symbol is thought to be an amalgam of a lightning bolt and an eagle's wing.

♄ *Saturn*

Nominative	Adjectival	Demonym
Saturn	Saturnian Saturnine	Saturnian
Kronos	Kronian	Kronian

The planet Saturn is named for Saturnus, Roman god of agriculture, bounty, renewal, liberation and wealth. The most famous of Roman festivals, Saturnalia, was a celebration of him, and it occurred during the dark part of the year, in December. It is this timing, between the death of the old year and the dawning of the new, that gave Saturnus association with the passage of time, and how he became related to the Greek Titan Kronos. The scythe that Saturnus carried to symbolize his relationship to the harvest became associated also with the passage of time and with death, hence the image of the Grim Reaper bearing a scythe to mow the souls of the dead. The planet's symbol represents the grisly blade.

♅ *Uranus*

Nominative	Adjectival	Demonym
Uranus	Uranian	Uranian

The planet Uranus was named for Οὐρανός *(Ouranos)*, the primal Greek god of the sky. Ouranos was both son and husband to Gaia, Mother Earth. She created him, and then, together, they created the Titans and ancestors to the Olympians and other Greek gods. The symbol of this pale green world is that of a globe with a ray pointed skyward.

♆ *Neptune*

Nominative	Adjectival	Demonym
Neptune	Neptunian	Neptunian
	Neptunial	

The Roman god Neptūnus, and his Greek counterpart Ποσειδῶν *(Poseidon)*, were the gods of water and the sea. The Greeks attributed both mælstroms and earthquakes to his wrath. It seems an appropriate name for this stormy world of ultramarine. Neptune's magical trident is the planet's symbol.

Dwarf Planets

In 2006, the IAU created the term *dwarf planet* to satisfy the perceived discrepancy between the nature of Pluto and the other eight planets. Like planets, dwarf planets have adjectival forms, too. The following section details the adjectivals and demonyms of each of the known dwarf planets, as well as a bit of background information for each body.

♇ *Pluto*

Nominative	Adjectival	Demonym
Pluto	Plutonian	Plutonian

Pluto was classified as a planet from its discovery by Clyde Tombaugh in 1930 until the IAU created the term *dwarf planet* in 2006. It is a small, icy body with five known satellites: Charon, Nix, Hydra, Kerberos, and Styx. An Earth probe will pass by Pluto in 2015 as part of the New Horizons mission to the Outer Solar System. It will be the first Earth craft to visit the Plutonian system. Pluto's astronomical symbol is a monogram of the first two letters of its name.

⚳ *Ceres*

Nominative	Adjectival	Demonym
Ceres	Cerenean	Cerenian

Ceres is the largest asteroid and the only dwarf planet in the Inner Solar System. It was discovered in

1801 by Giuseppe Piazzi, and, like Pluto, it was classified as a planet upon its discovery. Subsequent discoveries of other similar objects in the same region (later recognized as the asteroid belt between the orbits of Mars and Jupiter) caused astronomers to reconsider the planetary status of Ceres and the other objects in the region. It is named for Ceres, the Roman goddess of agriculture and grain, and from whose name we get the word *cereal*. Its astronomical symbol is a reaping hook.

Haumea

Nominative	Adjectival	Demonym
Haumea	Haumeaean	Haumean

Haumea is a dwarf planet and Kuiper belt object (KBO). It was discovered in 2004 at Palomar Observatory in California. The IAU recognized it as a dwarf planet in 2008, and it is named after the Hawaiian goddess of childbirth. The IAU often names objects in this region after Earth deities associated with birth and creation. One interesting and unique feature of Haumea is its shape. While its shape has not been directly observed, calculations based upon its light curve suggest that it is an ellipsoid, with the ratio of its major axis to its minor one being approximately 2:1.

Makemake

Nominative	Adjectival	Demonym
Makemake	Makemakean	Makemakian

Makemake, pronounced "maki-maki," is a dwarf planet and KBO that is about ⅔ the size of Pluto, making it one of the largest KBOs. It was discovered in 2005 at Palomar Observatory. Makemake is the creator god of the Rapanui, the people of Easter Island.

Eris

Nominative	Adjectival	Demonym
Eris	Eridian	Eridian

Eris is the most massive dwarf planet known. Discovered in 2005 at Palomar Observatory, Eris is named for Ἔρις *(Eris)*, a Greek allegory for strife and discord; the name was proposed because of the unsettling it caused in the way planets, KBOs and Trans-Neptunian Objects (TNOs) were classified. Its moon, Dysnomia, was named for Δυσνομία *(Dysnomia)*, the daughter of Eris and the personification of lawlessness in Greek mythology.

Chapter IV:

ADJECTIVALS

of

THE 88 CONSTELLATIONS

There are 88 constellations in the night sky. These 88 star patterns were derived arbitrarily over the ages, eventually culminating in the sky maps used by all astronomers today. Any star figure or pattern that is not one of the 88 is known as an *asterism*. Asterisms can be ancient or modern: you can even make one up yourself. Perhaps the most well-known asterism is the Big Dipper. Asterisms often are the brightest or most conspicuous portions of constellations, but not always.

Each constellation has a nominative form, English name (descriptor), genitive form, abbreviation, product adjectival, and independent adjectival forms. The nominative form is used when discussing the constellation itself. Genitive forms are used in Bayer star designations, such as in β Crucis (meaning "the Beta of Crux"), and abbreviations are also used in Bayer designation when space is at a premium. Product adjectives are used when discussing meteor showers, as the meteors appear to radiate from (or seem to be produced by) a given constellation (*e.g.* Orionid meteors). Independent adjectives are rarely used, but are included here for the sake of completion. The following section provides all word forms for each of the 88 constellations, plus some information about the constellation's background.

ANDROMEDA,
the Chained Maiden

Genitive	Abbr.	Prod. Adj.	Ind. Adj.
Andromedae	And	Andromedid	Andromedean

In Greek myth, Ἀνδρομέδα *(Andromeda)* was the daughter of Κηφεύς *(Cepheus)*, an Æthiopian king, and Κασσιόπεια *(Cassiopeia)*, both of whom also have constellations named for them. Cassiopeia's flaw was hubris, and thus she boasted far and wide that her daughter's beauty surpassed all, including the Nereids, the nymphs of the sea. Poseidon was so enraged by this that he sent a terrible sea monster to exact his wrath upon Æthiopia. In an effort to sate the monster, Andromeda was chained to a rock beside the raging sea as a sacrifice to Poseidon. She was saved in the nick of time by the hero Περσεύς *(Perseus)*, whom she later married and with whom she later departed eastward to Persia, the kingdom which he founded and which bears his name.

ANTLIA,
the Air Pump

Genitive	Abbr.	Prod. Adj.	Ind. Adj.
Antliae	Ant	Antlid	Antlian

Antlia is a faint constellation of the southern sky. It was created in 1756 by Nicolas Louis de Lacaille, a French astronomer who, in 1750, travelled to South Africa's Cape of Good Hope to observe the southern sky. He charted some 10,000 stars, and came up with southern constellations to fill in some fainter regions. Lacaille chose the air pump to commemorate the work of French physicist Denis Papin in the field of pneumatics. Papin lived from 1647 to about 1712. He worked with Christiaan Huygens and Gottfried Leibnitz in 1673, in Paris, where he became interested in using vacuums to generate motive power. From 1675 to 1679, Papin lived in London and worked with Robert Boyle (who originated Boyle's Law). It was during this time that Papin invented a device called a *steam digester*. It was a type of pressure cooker with a safety valve used to cook the fats out of bones so that they could be easily ground into meal. The steam digester was the forerunner of today's domestic pressure cookers, and Papin's work in pneumatics led to the development of the first steam engine by Thomas Savery in 1698.

APUS,
the Bird of Paradise

Genitive	Abbr.	Prod. Adj.	Ind. Adj.
Apodis	Aps	Apid	Apan

Apus is a southern constellation created around 1597 by Petrus Plancius, a Dutch astronomer, cartographer and clergyman. Plancius introduced eight new constellations on a small celestial globe published in Amsterdam by Pieter van der Keere. The figure we now call Apus was listed by Plancius as *Paradysvogel Apis Indica*. While the first word is Dutch for "bird of paradise," *Apis Indica* is Latin for "Indian Bee." Some scholars believe it was a misprinting, and that Plancius meant *avis*, meaning "bird." Interestingly, the name we use for the constellation today is derived from the Greek ἄπους *(apous)*, meaning "not foot," or "without feet." The Greeks used the term to refer to Sand Martins, migratory passerine birds in the swallow family, who make their homes in many windy holes in sandy hills throughout the world, and who rarely reveal their feet. The Bird of Paradise comes into the story in 1522, when survivors of Magellan's circumnavigational voyage brought back specimens of the birds with wings and feet removed. From this was reinforced a misconception in western Europe that Birds of Paradise had no feet at all.

AQUARIUS,
the Water Bearer

Genitive	Abbr.	Prod. Adj.	Ind. Adj.
Aquarii	Aqr	Aquariid	Aquarian

Aquarius is one of the oldest constellations in the night sky. In Babylonian star catalogues, he is identified as GU.LA "The Great One." He represents Ea, the Mesopotamian god of water and trickery, whose attribute is a great, overflowing vessel. Aquarius contained the southern solstice in the Early Bronze Age, and the Babylonians reviled him because of the destructive floods that occurred in the land between the rivers during this time. His reception was quite different in Egypt, where the Egyptians welcomed Aquarius to dip his jar into the Nile, bringing spring floods and fertility to the Valley.

AQUILA,
the Eagle

Genitive	Abbr.	Prod. Adj.	Ind. Adj.
Aquilae	Aql	Aquilid	Aquilean

Aquila is the sky eagle and one of the 48 constellations described by Ptolemy in the A.D. 2nd century. The figure is likely much older than that, as the Babylonians wrote of a sky eagle, called MUL.A.MUSHEN, that was located in the same general celestial region as Aquila today. In Ptolemy's time, there was a constellation called Antinous near Aquila. Though discarded in 1930 when the IAU formalized the constellations, Antinous was once an important constellation in the Roman world. It was created by the Roman Emperor Hadrian in A.D. 132. Hadrian once consulted an oracle who told him that the death of someone he held most dear would one day save him from grave danger. The oracle's prognostication came to be in 132 when, during an Egyptian expedition, Hadrian was saved from drowning in the Nile by Antinous, his boy favorite. After saving his friend, Antinous' strength failed, and the riparian flow carried him to the fields of Elysium. Hadrian, distraught with grief, named an asterism in memory of his departed friend, thus creating the ancient constellation of Antinous.

ARA,
the Altar

Genitive	Abbr.	Prod. Adj.	Ind. Adj.
Arae	Ara	Areid	Arean

Ara was one of Ptolemy's 48 constellations. In Greek mythology, the sky altar is where offerings were made when the Olympians first made their pact to overthrow the Titans. The nearby Milky Way can be seen as the smoke wafting up (although Ara appears upside down to northern hemisphere observers) from the burnt offerings. The youngest known planetary nebula is located within Ara, some 18,000 light years distant. Prior to the nebula's formation, the central star was known as He3-1357, an Hα (hydrogen-alpha) emission line star first cataloged by Karl Gordon Henize in 1967. It was found to be a protoplanetary nebula in 1971, and planetary nebula emission lines were detected there in 1989. An image of the nebula was first possible in 1994 with the great resolving power of the Hubble Space Telescope. Today, the nebula is known informally as the Stingray Nebula. [Bobrowsky]

ARIES,
the Ram

Genitive	Abbr.	Prod. Adj.	Ind. Adj.
Arietis	Ari	Arietid	Arian

Aries is Latin for "ram." The celestial ram is special in that its fleece became the fabled Golden Fleece, which was stolen by Ἰάσων καὶ Ἀργοναῦται *(Jason and the Argonauts)*.   Long ago, Ἀθάμας *(Athamas)* the Minyan took as his wife Νεφέλη *(Nephele)*, the goddess of the clouds. Athamas and Nephele had two children, a boy called Φρίξος *(Phrixus)* and a girl called Ἕλλη *(Helle)*. As is often the case, Athamas' eyes wandered, and his faithfulness to Nephele faltered. The goddess stormed away, and the land was scoured by terrible drought. Athamas took up with Ἰνώ *(Ino)*, Queen of Thebes, who was an evil stepmother to Phrixus and Helle. She made them toil in filth, and her cruelty reached its height when she plotted their deaths. Upon hearing of their peril, Nephele's spirit flew to her beloved children upon a magical, winged ram with golden fleece. The children, delighted to see their mother, jumped onto the golden ram and together they flew away over the sea. Tragically, Helle fell from the ram's back and drowned in the straight that now bears her name, Ἑλλήσποντος *(the Hellespont)*. The ram then spoke to Phrixus, calming him, and he took the boy to Κολχίς *(Colchis)* on the eastern shores of the Euxine (Black) Sea. It was there that Phrixus sacrificed the golden ram to Poseidon. The ram's spirit traveled to the sky and became the constellation Aries, but Phrixus saved the ram's golden fleece. Many years later, he gave the fleece to Αἰήτης *(Æëtes)*, king of Colchis, and father of Χαλκιόπη *(Chalciope)*, Phrixus' beloved, in exchange for the king's kindness. Æëtes took the golden fleece and hung it in a sacred oak grove, where it remained, guarded by a dragon, until Jason came and took it.

AURIGA,
the Charioteer

Genitive	Abbr.	Prod. Adj.	Ind. Adj.
Arigae	Aur	Aurigid	Aurigan

The Greek hero Ἐριχθόνιος *(Erichthonius)* of Athens is often associated with Auriga. Erichthonius is usually credited as the inventor of the quadriga, or four-horse chariot. The quadriga was first created in the image of Apollo's chariot, and thus Ζεύς *(Zeús)* honored Erichthonius by placing him into the night sky. The brightest star in this constellation is Capella. Its name is the diminutive form of Latin *capra*, meaning "female goat," so *capella* means, literally, "little female goat." Capella represented Amalthea, the she-goat that suckled young Jupiter in Roman myth. It was Amalthea's horn, after being accidentally broken off by the young god, that became the cornucopia: a magical horn that filled with whatever its bearer desired.

BOÖTES,
the Herdsman

Genitive	Abbr.	Prod. Adj.	Ind. Adj.
Boötis	Boo	Boötid	Boötian

Boötes is one of Ptolemy's 48 constellations, but it is much older than the *Almagest*. The constellation appears in Babylonian cuneiform tablets as SHU.PA. It was associated with Enlil, their chief deity, who was sacred to farmers. It is hard to say exactly who Boötes represents in Greek tradition.   One story has him as a farmer driving oxen, plowing the northern sky with the stars of the Big Dipper.   The Greeks sometimes called him Ἀρκτοφύλαξ *(Arctophylax)*, which means "Bear Watcher," for he minded the bears Καλλιστώ (Callisto) and Ἀρκάς *(Arcas)*, the transfigured bodies of Zeus' lover and her son.   Arcturus, the fourth brightest star in Earth's sky, resides in Boötes.   Its name comes from the Greek ἄρκτος *(arktos)*, meaning "bear."

CÆLUM,
the Engraving Chisel

Genitive	Abbr.	Prod. Adj.	Ind. Adj.
Cæli	Cæ	Cælid	Cælan

The Chisel is a southern constellation created by Lacaille in 1756.   It is incredibly faint, having no star above fourth magnitude.   Lacaille called it *les Burins*, meaning "Chisel" in French.   It was later changed to Latin *Cæla Sculptoris*, "the sculptor's chisel," and the short form, *Cælum*, was adopted when the IAU formalized the constellations in 1930.   Alpha Cæli, the constellation's brightest star at apparent magnitude +4.44, is most likely part of the Ursa Major Moving Group, a set of stars with common velocities and (possibly) common origins that includes most of the stars of the Big Dipper (minus Alkaid and Dubhe). [King, et al.]

CAMELOPARDALIS,
the Giraffe

Genitive	Abbr	Prod. Adj.	Ind. Adj.
Camelopardalis	Cam	Camelopardalid	Camelopardalian

Like Apus, Camelopardalis is attributed to Petrus Plancius, who, in 1597 published a small celestial globe in Amsterdam featuring eight new constellations. The word *camelopardalis* is a Romanized portmanteau of two Greek words: κάμηλος *(kamēlos)*, meaning "camel," and πάρδαλις *(pardalis)*, meaning "leopard." The name came from the fact that the giraffe had a long neck like a camel and spots resembling those of a leopard. Kemble's Cascade is an asterism found in Camelopardalis. It is a beautiful train of 20 or so stars of many colors with the open cluster NGC 1502 at one end. Walter Scott Houston wrote an article in the December 1980 issue of *Sky & Telescope* describing the asterism. Houston had learned of the asterism in a letter from Franciscan friar and amateur astronomer Father Lucian Kemble. Kemble noted the asterism's beauty one night as he swept the area of Camelopardalis with a pair of 7x35 binoculars. Houston called the new asterism "Kemble's Cascade" in his article, and the name stuck. [Houston]

CANCER,
the Crab

Genitive	Abbr.	Prod. Adj.	Ind. Adj.
Cancri	Can	Cancrid	Cancerian

One of the twelve constellations of the zodiac, Cancer's name means "crab" in Latin. It commonly represents the crab that crawled from the sea, biting Herakles' foot during his fateful battle with the Lernaean Hydra during the second of his twelve labors. Herakles crushed the crab under foot, and Hera placed it into the heavens to spite him. The wondrous Beehive Cluster lies directly in the crab's belly. Its Latin name, *Præsepe*, means "manger." Galileo was fascinated by the Beehive, and he was able to see about 40 stars there when he trained his telescope on it in 1609.

CANES VENATICI,
the Hunting Dogs

Genitive	Abbr.	Prod. Adj.	Ind. Adj.
Canum Venaticorum	CVn	Canum Venaticorid	Canum Venatician

Canes Venatici was created by Johannes Hevelius in 1687. The constellation's name means "hunting dogs" in Latin, and they are usually depicted as the hunting dogs of Boötes. Canes Venatici is famous as the home of the Whirlpool Galaxy (M51). Discovered in 1773 by Charles Messier, and listed as the 51st object on his list, the Whirlpool Galaxy was not recognized as a spiral object until 1845, when it was observed by Lord Rosse, with his 72-inch reflector, at Birr Castle in Ireland. Lord Rosse was the first person to observe spiral galactic structure in any celestial object.

CANIS MAJOR,
the Greater Dog

Genitive	Abbr.	Prod. Adj.	Ind. Adj.
Canis Majoris	CMa	Canis Majorid	Canis Majoran

Orion's large hunting dog was one of Ptolemy's 48 constellations. The constellation contains Sirius, the brightest star in the night sky. Canis Major is the only sky dog spoken of in Hellenic legend. Sometimes he was imagined as Λαῖλαψ *(Lælaps)*, a hound who never failed to capture his quarry. Lælaps found himself in the midst of a paradox when Ἀμφιτρύων *(Amphitryon)* set him upon Τευμησία ἀλώπηξ *(Teumēsiā alôpēx, the Teumessian fox)*, a magical fox that could never be caught. Lælaps chased the fox tirelessly until Zeus, having enough of their exclusive relationship, turned them both to stone and cast them into the stars.

CANIS MINOR,
the Lesser Dog

Genitive	Abbr.	Prod. Adj.	Ind. Adj.
Canis Minoris	CMi	Canis Minorid	Canis Minoran

The little sky dog is marked by the two relatively bright stars Procyon and Gomeisa. Canis Minor's origins can be traced back to around 1100 B.C., when the ancient Mesopotamians called its bright stars MASH.TAB.BA ("twins") on the *Three Stars Each* tablets. The Greeks often associated the stars of Canis Minor with the Teumessian fox.

CAPRICORNUS,
the Sea Goat

Genitive	Abbr.	Prod. Adj.	Ind. Adj.
Capricorni	Cap	Capricornid	Capricornian

Representing a mythical composite of half goat, half fish, Capricornus is also one of the 12 zodiac constellations. In addition, it was one of the 48 constellations listed by Ptolemy in the *Almagest*. Though it is quite faint, this constellation is among the oldest, having been identified since at least the Middle Bronze Age. The Sea Goat was sometimes imagined as the goat Ἀμάλθεια *(Amalthea)*, who suckled the infant Zeus after he was saved from being devoured by his father Κρόνος *(Kronos)*.

CARINA,
the Keel

Genitive	Abbr.	Prod. Adj.	Ind. Adj.
Carinae	Car	Carinid	Carinean

Carina marks the keel of *Argo Navis*, the Ship of the Argonauts, which was once a constellation in its own right before being split into three parts in modern times. Ἀργώ *(Argo)* means "swift" in Ancient Greek, and it was the name of the ship used by Jason on his quest for the Golden Fleece. Canopus, its brightest star, is second only to Sirius in brilliance as viewed from Earth. This supergiant derives its name from the Greek Κάνωβος *(Kanôbos)*, who was pilot for Μενέλαος *(Menelaus)* of Sparta, husband to Helen of Troy.

CASSIOPEIA,
the Seated Queen

Genitive	Abbr.	Prod. Adj.	Ind. Adj.
Cassiopeiae	Cas	Cassiopeiid	Cassiopeian

Κασσιόπεια *(Cassiopeia)* was the mythological queen of Æthiopia, wife of Κηφεύς *(Cepheus)* and mother of Ἀνδρομέδα *(Andromeda)*. As punishment for her boasting (see Andromeda's entry above), she was placed into the sky upon her throne into a region near the north celestial pole. There, she was forced to wheel ceaselessly about the pole: half the time having to cling tightly to her throne to keep from falling.

CENTAURUS,
the Centaur

Genitive	Abbr.	Prod. Adj.	Ind. Adj.
Centauri	Cen	Centaurid	Centaurian

The sky centaur's lineage can be traced back to ancient Babylon, where he was known as a strange creature called MUL.GUD.ALIM, the bison-man. He was closely associated with the sun god Utu-Shamash. Shamash was said to have bestowed the Code to Hammurabi, Sixth King of Babylon, where he made it decree sometime around 1772 B.C., making it the earliest known law code in human history. Centaurus was also one of Ptolemy's 48 constellations.

CEPHEUS,
the King

Genitive	Abbr.	Prod. Adj.	Ind. Adj.
Cephei	Cep	Cepheid	Chephean

Κηφεύς *(Cepheus)* was an Æthiopian king in the Perseus myth. He was father to Ἀνδρομέδα *(Andromeda)* and husband to Κασσιόπεια *(Cassiopeia)*. Ptolemy listed him in the *Almagest* as one of the 48 constellations. The prototype Cepheid variable star, δ Cephei, is found within this constellation. It is one of the closest stars to Sol of this type.

CETUS,
the Sea Monster

Genitive	Abbr.	Prod. Adj.	Ind. Adj.
Ceti	Cet	Cetid	Cetan

Κῆτος *(Kētos, Cetus)* is the sea monster dispatched by Poseidon to ravage Æthiopia in the Perseus myth. He met his end by petrification when presented with the severed head of Μέδουσα *(Medusa)* by Περσεύς *(Perseus)*, who had recently slain the gorgon. Cetus exists in a region of the sky often called "The Sea" in ancient times, due to the large number of hydrophilic constellations found there, such as Aquarius, Capricornus, Eridanus, Pisces and Piscis Austrinus.

CHAMÆLEON,
the Chameleon

Genitive	Abbr.	Prod. Adj.	Ind. Adj.
Chamæleontis	Cha	Chamæleontid	Chamæleonian

Petrus Plancius created the Chameleon on a small celestial globe he published around 1597, in Amsterdam. It was one of several constellations created during the Age of Discovery, when Europeans began to encounter the unfamiliar stars of the southern sky. It is home to the Chamæleon Complex, a large star forming region dominated by three dark clouds, Chamæleon I, Chamæleon II and Chamæleon III, which nearly fill the constellation's boundaries. Chamæleon II contains Uhuru Source 4U 1302-77, an X-ray source discovered by the Uhuru satellite, first X-ray observatory satellite. The Uhuru Satellite was launched in 1970 and analyzed X-ray radiation from several sources, including Cygnus X-1, the first strong black hole candidate.

CIRCINUS,
the (Draftsman's) Compass

Genitive	Abbr.	Prod. Adj.	Ind. Adj.
Circini	Cir	Circinid	Circinian

Circinus is a faint southern constellation that was created by Lacaille in 1756. It represents a draftsman's compass, and therefore care should be used to avoid confusion with the constellation Pyxis, the Mariner's Compass. Lacaille included Circinus, Norma and Triangulum Australe as a draftsman's tool set of compass, level and set square on his star map. Circinus is home to the Circinus Galaxy (ESO 97-G13). It is a small spiral galaxy about 26,000 light years in diameter and about 14 million light years away from Sol. It lies just 4° off the plane of the Milky Way and is relatively unobscured by gas and dust: an oddity given its relative position. ESO 97-G13 has an active nucleus, with jets of gas erupting along its rotational pole line as matter falls onto the supermassive black hole at its heart. [Maiolino, et al.]

COLUMBA,
the Dove

Genitive	Abbr.	Prod. Adj.	Ind. Adj.
Columbae	Col	Columbid	Columbean

The sky dove was first described by Plancius in 1597. It is a small, faint constellation just south of Canis Major. Plancius' original name was *Columba Noachi*, meaning "Noah's Dove" in Latin, and referring to the dove sent out by Noah to search for dry land after the Great Flood. Phact (α Columbae) and Wazn (β Columbae) were traditionally known as the "Good Messengers" or "Bringers of Good News." *Phact* comes from Arabic for "Ring Dove," referring to the Eurasian Collared Dove, which has a black ring-like pattern on its neck. *Wazn*, comes from *al-Wazn*, which is Arabic for "weight."

COMA BERENICES,
the Hair of Queen Berenice

Genitive	Abbr.	Prod. Adj.	Ind. Adj.
Comae Berenices	Com	Comae Berenicid	Comae Berenician

Coma Berenices is unusual among the constellations, as it is one of only two that are associated with historical figures. Queen Berenice II of Egypt was the wife of Ptolemy III Euergetes, the king of Alexandria from 246-221 B.C., and under whose rule Alexandria rose to great cultural prominence. In 243 B.C., Ptolemy

III went on a dangerous quest against the Seleucids during the Third Syrian War. To help safeguard her husband, Queen Berenice sacrificed her beautiful, long blonde hair to Aphrodite. She cut off her flowing locks and placed them upon the altar in the temple. The next morning, the hair had vanished! The king was incensed, and, to appease him, Conon, the court astronomer, proclaimed that the hair had so pleased the goddess that she saw fit to put it into the night sky. That night, Conon gestured skyward, pointing out the stars of Coma Berenices to the king, and so we have imagined them as the Queen's marvelous hair ever since.

CORONA AUSTRALIS,
the Southern Crown

Genitive	Abbr.	Prod. Adj.	Ind. Adj.
Coronae Australis	CrA	Coronae Australid	Coronae Australian

The Southern Crown is often imagined as the laurel crown of the centaur archer Sagittarius. The African Bushmen of the Kalahari call it ≠*nabbe ta !nu*, meaning "house of branches." Strange as it may be to Western eyes and ears, this language is called |xam. The bars and exclamation point represent dental clicks, perhaps the most renowned of the language's traits. In any case, this "house of branches" was the home of the Dassie, the rock hyrax. It is said that the people came there, and that they sat around a fire, in a half circle, eating delicious food. A beautiful maiden appeared in the Dassie's house, and the people became transfixed. The maiden's charm was so powerful that all the people, the

Dassie - even the house and the fire - were turned to stars, and we see them still today, sitting in the half circle in the night sky.

CORONA BOREALIS,
the Northern Crown

Genitive	Abbr.	Prod. Adj.	Ind. Adj.
Coronae Borealis	CrB	Coronae Borealid	Coronae Borealian

The Northern Crown was one of Ptolemy's 48 constellations. The Greeks saw it as the nuptial crown that was given to Ἀριάδνη *(Ariadne)* by Διόνυσος *(Dionysus)* the god of grapes and wine. The Welsh called it *Caer Arianrhod*, "the Castle of the Silver Wheel." It was there that Lady Arianrhod, sister of Gwydion dwelled. The castle is associated with a rock formation visible in northeast Wales, off the shores of Gwynedd, whose coastline resembles the pattern of Corona Borealis in the northern sky.

CORVUS,
the Crow

Genitive	Abbr.	Prod. Adj.	Ind. Adj.
Corvi	Cor	Corvid	Corvan

A constellation of the southern sky, and one of Ptolemy's 48 constellations, Corvus is the Greek interpretation of the Babylonian Raven, MUL.UGA.MUSHEN. The Raven was a familiar of Adad, to whom it was sacred. Adad was the Babylonian god of storms and rain, and in their time Corvus rose in the east just before the start of the fall rainy season. The four brightest stars of Corvus form the asterism known as Spica's Spanker. A spanker is a type of sail, and this particular one is formed by connecting β, γ, δ and ε Corvi. A line drawn between γ and δ Corvi point to the star Spica.

CRATER,
the Cup

Genitive	Abbr.	Prod. Adj.	Ind. Adj.
Crateris	Crt	Craterid	Craterian

Another Greek tale involving Corvus, the Crow includes Crater, as well. Legend has it that Apollo sent the crow with a cup after water to sate his tremendous thirst. Instead of going directly to the spring and filling the cup, the crow lolly-gagged, stopping along the way to eat figs. When the crow finally returned, Apollo asked why he had been delayed. The crow lied, saying that a water snake had blocked the spring. The bird must have been a terrible liar, as Apollo could see through his deceit, and so he smacked the crow so hard that both bird and cup flew into the sky, where they remained forevermore.

CRUX,
the Southern Cross

Genitive	Abbr.	Prod. Adj.	Ind. Adj.
Crucis	Cru	Crucid	Crucian

What this famous constellation lacks in size (it is the smallest of the 88 modern constellations), it makes up for in distinctiveness. The Southern Cross is a symbol of exotic places, strange vistas, and the thrill of exploration. The ancient Greeks knew it as part of Centaurus, and it was visible as far north as Britain in the fourth millennium B.C, but the precession of the equinoxes gradually lowered it to the point where, by A.D. 400, it never rose above the southern horizon in Europe, even as far south as the Peloponnese. It came back into European consciousness during the Age of Discovery, when explorers like Pedro Álvares Cabral and Amerigo Vespucci came back from the New World with drawings of it on their charts. The principal stars of Crux now appear on the banners of five southern nations: Australia, Brazil, New Zealand, Papua New Guinea, and Samoa.

CYGNUS,
the Swan

Genitive	Abbr.	Prod. Adj.	Ind. Adj.
Cygni	Cyg	Cygnid	Cygnian

There are many swans in the mists of legend. The sky swan flies near Lyra, the Lyre, and a tale that involves them both is that of Ὀρφεύς *(Orpheus)*, the legendary prophetic bard, whose music was so beautiful that it could charm all things. The tale of Orpheus and his wife Εὐρυδίκη *(Eurydikē, Eurydice)* is perhaps the most heart-breaking in human history. Orpheus and Eurydice were madly in love, but on their wedding day, tragedy struck. On that fateful day, a satyr appeared and chased Eurydice. In her flight, she fell into a nest of vipers and was fatally bitten. Orpheus was devastated. His mournful songs wafted throughout the world, and it was said that all creatures under heaven wept with him. The passion of Orpheus' music stirred even the gods to tears, and so it was decided that he should be allowed to venture into the underworld to find Eurydice and bring her back to the world of the living. Hades never allowed spirits to leave the underworld, but when Orpheus found Eurydice, he played his lyre and sang of his undying love for her. The beautiful music softened Hades' heart, and he allowed Orpheus to leave with Eurydice on one condition: that as they left the underworld, he should lead and not look back until they had reached the overworld. Orpheus set off immediately with his bride, but, upon reaching the overworld, he looked back in anxiety to see if his beloved followed, and Eurydice was lost forever. Death eventually freed Orpheus of his grief, when, after the spark of life left him, he was changed into a swan who flies through the celestial ribbons of the Milky Way. The tale of Orpheus and Eurydice is a familiar one. It is an allegory for lost love, which often returns in dreams, but, upon waking, is gone forever, leaving behind only the crushing heartbreak of lonesome reality.

DELPHINUS,
the Dolphin

Genitive	Abbr.	Prod. Adj.	Ind. Adj.
Delphini	Del	Delphinid	Delphinian

The Dolphin was in the *Almagest* as one of Ptolemy's 48 constellations. Its name literally means "dolphin" in Latin. The Greeks told a story about a poet named Ἀρίων *(Arion)* of the Isle of Lesbos. Arion was court musician to Περίανδρος *(Periander)*, the second king at Κόρινθος *(Kórinthos, Corinth)*. With his great talent, he traveled far and wide throughout the Mediterranean, even going as far abroad as Italy, Sicily and Sardinia. Arion's fame allowed him to amass tremendous wealth, which attracted the attention of all sorts of unsavory lots. After many successful trips, fortune abandoned Arion on a homeward voyage from Tarentum, when his ship was accosted by pirates. The pirates boarded Arion's ship, and, with a dagger to his throat, Arion begged for one last wish: to sing his own dirge. The crew laughed at this seemingly ridiculous request, and so granted it. As Arion began to sing, dolphins nearby became charmed by his magnificent music, and one leapt skyward just as Arion flung himself from the ship, allowing him to ride on its back to safety. We can still see Arion riding the dolphin through the night sky if we look closely for the star ζ Delphini.

DORADO,
the Swordfish

Genitive	Abbr.	Prod. Adj.	Ind. Adj.
Doradus	Dor	Doradid	Doradan

While it is often called a swordfish, *dorado* means "dolphinfish" in Spanish. Dolphinfish are delicious, especially when filleted and grilled with lime and then served in a sandwich with fries and ice cold beer. In the Carolinas, Georgia and Florida, dolphinfish is usually referred to simply as "dolphin," which can cause confusion amongst visitors, who usually first think of the cetacean when hearing the word. Dolphinfish are also called *mahi-mahi*, which is 'Ōlelo Hawai'i for "very strong." In one of those cosmic coincidences, *mahi* means "fish" in Persian.

DRACO,
the Dragon

Genitive	Abbr.	Prod. Adj.	Ind. Adj.
Draconis	Dra	Draconid	Draconian

Containing the star α Draconis, or Thuban, which was the Pole Star during the time of the ancient Egyptians, Draco glides deftly about the circumpolar region. The word *thuban* is Arabic for snake, and the star will again be Earth's northern pole star by the year A.D. 21000. The Greeks often imagined Draco as the dragon Λάδων *(Ladon)*, who was ever entwined about the tree in the Garden of the Hesperides, guarding the golden apples there. Ladon was overcome by Herakles during his quest for the apples as the eleventh of his Twelve Labors. In amazing coincidence, legend has it that Jason and the Argonauts passed by there the very next day on their return voyage for the Golden Fleece, when they heard the shrieking lament of Αἴγλη *(Aegle)*, one of the four Hesperides, at the theft of the golden apples and the slaughter of Ladon. It is said that Jason came ashore and looked upon the dragon's still-twitching carcass.

EQUULEUS,
the Little Horse

Genitive	Abbr.	Prod. Adj.	Ind. Adj.
Equulei	Equ	Equulid	Equulian

Ptolemy listed this constellation in his *Almagest*. Its name is Latin for "little horse," or "foal." It is the second smallest among the 88 modern constellations. Equuleus is most often imagined as Κέλερες *(Celeris)*, the brother of Pegasus, and they appear near one another in the sky. According to the Roman poet Ovid, Celeris was given to Castor by the god Mercurius. The Romans often called this star pattern *Equus Primus*, "the First Horse," as it rises slightly before Pegasus.

ERIDANUS,
the River

Genitive	Abbr.	Prod. Adj.	Ind. Adj.
Eridani	Eri	Eridanid	Eridanian

A long stellar meander of the southern sky, Eridanus was one of Ptolemy's original 48 constellations. At its southern terminus is brilliant Achernar, whose name comes from Arabic and means "the river's end." The Babylonians described a constellation known as MUL.NUN.KI, which they called the Star of Eridu. Eridu was a mysterious ancient city in the far southern reaches of Babylonia, surrounded by marsh. It was said to be sacred to Enki-Ea, god of the Abyss, the vast freshwater reservoir that was believed to exist underneath the earth.

FORNAX,
the Furnace

Genitive	Abbr.	Prod. Adj.	Ind. Adj.
Fornacis	For	Fornacid	Fornacian

Fornax is a faint constellation in the southern sky created by the Frenchman Lacaille in 1756. He originally named it *Fornax Chemica*, meaning "chemical furnace" in Latin. It contains some interesting deep-sky objects, including the Fornax Dwarf, a dwarf elliptical galaxy orbiting the Milky Way, that was discovered by Harlow Shapley in 1938. The Fornax Dwarf has six globular clusters and it is quite faint at magnitude +9.3.

The Hubble Ultra-Deep Field, which looks back approximately 13 billion years, is also within Fornax.

GEMINI,
the Twins

Genitive	Abbr.	Prod. Adj.	Ind. Adj.
Geminorum	Gem	Geminid	Geminorian

In Ancient Babylon, the two brightest stars of this constellation were called "the Great Twins, or MUL.MASH.TAB.BA.GAL.GAL. In Greece, these stellar twins were known as Κάστωρ καὶ Πολυδεύκης *(Castor and Polydeuces/Pollux)*. Their mother was Λήδα *(Leda)*, the wife of Τυνδάρεως *(Tyndareus)*, the king of Sparta. Leda was much admired by Zeus, for she was virtuous and very beautiful. In the form of a swan, he fell into her arms one day to escape an eagle's talons. There, the swan seduced Leda and left within her his immortal seed. That night, her husband, Tyndareus, laid with her also, and the result of the two consummations was four fertilized eggs. Castor and Κλυταιμνήστρα *(Clytemnestra)* were being born from eggs fertilized by Tyndareus, while Pollux and Ἑλένη *(Helénē)* were born from the eggs graced by Zeus' immortal touch. (This Helénē became the famous Helen of Troy.) Much later, when Castor was killed, Zeus offered Pollux a choice of living upon Mount Olympus forever, or giving up half of his immortality to resurrect his brother. Pollux chose life for Castor, and so they were transformed and placed among the stars, spending half their time upon Olympus, in the sky, and half in the underworld with Hades.

GRUS,
the Crane

Genitive	Abbr.	Prod. Adj.	Ind. Adj.
Gruis	Gru	Gruid	Gruian

The Crane was introduced by Plancius in the late 16th century. The stars in Grus were originally the tail of Piscis Austrinus. The star name Al Dhanab (γ Gruis), means "the tail" in Arabic. In the 17th century, the constellation was sometimes called Phoenicopterus, which is Latin for "flamingo."

HERCULES,
the Hero

Genitive	Abbr.	Prod. Adj.	Ind. Adj.
Herculis	Her	Herculid	Herculean

Many volumes could be filled telling the exploits of Hercules, but one tale in particular has to do with how we see him among the stars. The Greeks called him Ἡρακλῆς *(Hēraklēs)*. The brightest star in his constellation is Rasalgethi or Ras Algethi, which means "Head of the Kneeler" in Arabic. When Herakles passed through Liguria after his tenth labor, he encountered two fearsome giants, Ἀλεβίων *(Alebion)* and Βεργίων *(Bergion)*. Herakles knelt and prayed to his father Zeus for aid. Zeus answered his son's prayer and bestowed upon him his aegis, or breastplate, which protected him and allowed him to emerge victorious. Herakles' prayer is immortalized in this constellation, which the Greeks called Ἐγγόνασιν, "the Kneeler," which comes from ἐν γόνασιν, which means "on his knees."

HOROLOGIUM,
the Clock

Genitive	Abbr.	Prod. Adj.	Ind. Adj.
Horologii	Hor	Horologid	Horologian

Lacaille named this southern constellation in 1756. It was originally listed as Horologium Oscillitorium, or "Oscillating [pendulum] Clock," in honor of Dutch astronomer and mathematician Christiaan Huygens, who invented the device in 1656. It is a remarkable constellation in that not very many remarkable things are known to exist within its boundaries. One thing worth mentioning, though, is the globular cluster Arp-Madore 1, which is notable for being the most remote globular cluster known in the Milky Way, at a distance of about 400,000 light years. [Madore & Arp]

HYDRA,
the Female Water Snake

Genitive	Abbr.	Prod. Adj.	Ind. Adj.
Hydrae	Hya	Hydriid	Hydrean

It is easy to imagine a snake-like figure in the sky. Anyone can meander about the stars to pick one out, but there are three official serpents on our modern star maps. This particular snake is the same one that appears in the story with Apollo, the crow and the cup, and she appears just below them in the southern sky. Alpha

Hydrae, traditionally known as Alphard, is an orange giant whose name means "the solitary one" in Arabic. It is a fitting name, as it is the only bright star in the region. Another named star is Minaruja (σ Hydrae), whose Arabic name means "the snake's nose." A neat deep sky object in Hydra is NGC 3242, a planetary nebula known as the "Ghost of Jupiter" because of its uncanny resemblance to the giant planet when viewed through a small telescope. It was discovered by William Herschel in 1785.

HYDRUS,
the Male Water Snake

Genitive	Abbr.	Prod. Adj.	Ind. Adj.
Hydri	Hyd	Hydrid	Hydrian

Named by Petrus Plancius in 1597, and not to be confused with Hydra, the female water snake, Hydrus is her male counterpart. He must wander far through the environs of the celestial river, Eridanus, past Orion and through the Milky Way to woo his consort. The subgiant β Hydri is a star of approximately 1.08 solar masses and 1.81 solar diameters, being slightly more evolved than our parent star. [Brandão, et al.] Such a condition makes β Hydri a star of great interest to astronomers, as it represents a window into Sol's future, and thus our own.

INDUS,
the Indian

Genitive	Abbr.	Prod. Adj.	Ind. Adj.
Indi	Ind	Indiid	Indian

Indus was also created by Plancius in the late 16th century. It lies in the southern sky, and, like the others he created, is based upon observations of the southern sky made by explorers Pieter Dirkszoon Keyser and Frederick de Houtman. It represents a native of the New World, standing with arrows grasped in one hand. Epsilon Indi is a star not too far away from our own, being about 12 light years distant. Heinrich Louis d'Arrest noted its proper motion in 1847 by carefully comparing its position in star charts dating back to 1750. It is a ternary star system composed of a K-type main-sequence star and two brown dwarfs. Additionally, ε Indi is a star system of great interest to SETI astronomers due to its age, vicinity and iron content. [Stahl] If sentient life exists there, it could look into the night sky and see Sol near the Big Dipper's bowl, shining at magnitude +2.

LACERTA,
the Lizard

Genitive	Abbr.	Prod. Adj.	Ind. Adj.
Lacertae	Lac	Lacertid	Lacertan

Lacerta was created by Hevelius in 1687. It represents a lizard in the northern sky. BL Lacertae is the prototype of the eponymous class of objects. BL Lacertae is a type of elliptical galaxy with an active nucleus that exhibits large fluctuations in energy output, leading astronomers to first hypothesize that such objects were variable stars. Continued observations revealed them to be quasar-like, being differentiated by their spectra, which, unlike quasars, do not exhibit strong emission lines. [Stein, et al.]

LEO,
the Lion

Genitive	Abbr.	Prod. Adj.	Ind. Adj.
Leonis	Leo	Leonid	Leonian

Leo's very name means "lion" in Latin. Though the Romans certainly recognized the star pattern as being reminiscent of a lion, such recognition goes back much further, at least to the Mesopotamians of around 4000 B.C. The later Persians called Leo *Ser* or *Shir*, depending upon dialect or translation. Further east, in India, he was known as *Simha*, which shares similarity to the Swahili word *simba*, which means "lion," and is a name shared with Disney's eponymous Lion King. Speaking of kings, the Babylonians knew the sky lion as UR.GU.LA, "the Great Lion," which then contained the summer solstice. They also called the bright star we know as Regulus, LUGAL, which means "the star that stands in the breast of the Lion: the King."

LEO MINOR,
the Lesser Lion

Genitive	Abbr.	Prod. Adj.	Ind. Adj.
Leonis Minoris	LMi	Leonis Minorid	Leonis Minoran

The stars of Leo Minor belonged to no constellation until 1687, when Hevelius designated them as the "little lion" on his star map. In the *Almagest*, Ptolemy listed this area as ἀμωρφτοι (*amorphōtoi*), meaning "shapeless." Hevelius chose the name *Leo Minor* to create symmetry with the Greater and Lesser Bears that resided nearby.

LEPUS,
the Hare

Genitive	Abbr.	Prod. Adj.	Ind. Adj.
Leporis	Lep	Leporid	Leporian

Although the Hare does not represent any particular figure in Greek mythology, it was one of the constellations on Ptolemy's list. It nicely complements the scene with Orion and his hunting dogs just to the north. The second magnitude star Arneb (α Leporis) derives its name for "hare" in Arabic.

LIBRA,
the Scales

Genitive	Abbr.	Prod. Adj.	Ind. Adj.
Librae	Lib	Librid	Librean

Libra is unique among the zodiac constellations in that it is the only one that does not represent an animal. The stars in Libra once also represented the claws of Scorpius, and so it contains the stars Zubenelgenubi and Zubeneschamali, whose Arabic names mean "the southern claw" and "the northern claw," respectively. The Babylonians called it MUL.Z(ibanu), and it was known as both "the scales" and "Claws of the Scorpion." The scales were sacred to Shumash, god and patron of truth and justice. We see the influence of Shumash carrying on in our own society in the allegorical figure of Lady Justice (Latin *Iustitia*), who is depicted as holding the scales.

LUPUS,
the Wolf

Genitive	Abbr.	Prod. Adj.	Ind. Adj.
Lupi	Lup	Lupid	Lupian

Ptolemy listed the Wolf in the *Almagest*, but the star pattern was not associated as such in prior sources. Babylonian cuneiform tablets refer to this constellation as UR.DIM, otherwise referenced as a creature called the "Mad Dog." It is believed to have not been a dog, as such, but a composite beast with the head and torso of a man and the legs and hind parts of a lion or some other ferocious carnivore, as the cuneiform sign UR often referred to lions, but it can also represent bears, dogs and wolves.

LYNX,

the Lynx

Genitive	Abbr.	Prod. Adj.	Ind. Adj.
Lyncis	Lyn	Lyncid	Lyncian

The lynx is a wild cat known to some American Indians as the "keeper of secrets." He is mysterious and elusive: a creature of the night with brilliantly luminous eyes. The Greeks believed him to have supernatural eyesight, being able to see in perfect darkness and even through solid objects. It is because of these qualities that Hevelius organized some faint stars in the northern sky into this constellation, because only those with the vision of a lynx would be able to see it.

LYRA,

the Lyre

Genitive	Abbr.	Prod. Adj.	Ind. Adj.
Lyrae	Lyr	Lyrid	Lyrean

In Greek tradition, the lyre was often depicted as being carried by an eagle. After Orpheus was killed, his lyre was thrown into the river. Zeus sent an eagle to retrieve it, and upon its return to Olympus, Zeus placed both the eagle and the lyre in the sky. Welsh tradition refers to Lyra as *Talyn Arthur*, "King Arthur's Harp."

MENSA,
the Table Mountain

Genitive	Abbr.	Prod. Adj.	Ind. Adj.
Mensae	Men	Mensid	Mensean

Table Mountain is a flat-topped mountain overlooking the city of Cape Town in South Africa. It is an indelible symbol of Cape Town, and visitors can ride a cable car to its summit to enjoy what is often described as one of the most epic views in all of Africa. The seas around Cape Town are known for their tempestuousness, and the Arabic folk hero Sinbad the Sailor regarded Table Mountain as a magnet that pulled ships into the abyss. The Frenchman Lacaille studied the southern sky from the Cape, in the shadow of table mountain, and it was the mountain's notoriety as an iconic feature of the southern hemisphere that led Lacaille to create this constellation out of an obscure group of southern stars in 1756.

MICROSCOPIUM,
the Microscope

Genitive	Abbr.	Prod. Adj.	Ind. Adj.
Microscopii	Mic	Microscopid	Microscopian

Microscopium represents an 18th century microscope, an important tool in the scientific revolution occurring during that period. It was designated as such by Lacaille in 1756, both to commemorate scientific advances, and because of the star figure's similarity to its namesake. The G-type giant γ Microscopii is the brightest star in the constellation, but it is still quite faint at apparent magnitude +4.68. Measurements of its proper motion suggest that it may be part of the Ursa Major Moving Group, and that 3.8 million years ago, only six light years would have separated it from Sol. [King, et al.] Back then, γ Microscopii would have shone brilliantly at about magnitude -3 in Earth's sky.

MONOCEROS,
the Unicorn

Genitive	Abbr.	Prod. Adj.	Ind. Adj.
Monocerotis	Mon	Monocerotid	Monocerotean

This constellation represents a unicorn, and its name comes from the Greek word for that mythic animal. It was a favorite constellation of the late Robert Rood, a much-beloved astronomy professor at the University of Virginia. Though it has a Greek name, it is not ancient, being first described on Plancius' globe in the late 16th century. Monoceros may be a dim constellation, but many remarkable things may be found within it. The wondrous ternary star β Monocerotis is made up of three blue giants, which, as William Herschel remarked in 1781, is "one of the most beautiful sights in the heavens." Epsilon Monocerotis is beautiful in small telescopes, too, being a binary composed of one F-type and one A-type star. Perhaps the most striking object of all is V838 Monocerotis, a ruby-red variable star about 19,570 light years away from Sol. In early January, 2002, astronomers saw V838 Monocerotis brighten intensely. At first, it was thought to be a typical nova eruption, where matter from a companion star falls onto a white dwarf and explodes, generating a momentary flash of light. Something was different in this case, though, as later on, in March, the star flared up again, this time in infrared light. Another infrared flare-up was recorded in April before the star returned to its original luminosity. The light curve of V838 Monocerotis was quite queer indeed, being something that had never before been witnessed in astronomy. Hypotheses as to its nature abounded, including the thermal pulse of a dying star [Tylenda, et al.], a mergeburst (where two stars merge) [Soker, et al.] or a planetary capture (in this case, where giant planets would have become one with their parent star). [Retter, et al.] Many of these possibilities could have triggered fusion in the stellar envelope of V838 Monocerotis, possibly causing the outburst, but the exact nature of the event remains unclear. Whatever it was, the event caused an unprecedented and dazzling light echo that bounced off of gas and dust behind the star and was captured in a series of images by the Hubble Space Telescope from 2002-2004, providing excellent documentation of this strange event and its aftermath.

MUSCA,
the Fly

Genitive	Abbr.	Prod. Adj.	Ind. Adj.
Muscae	Mus	Muscid	Muscean

Musca was originally named Apis, the Bee. Isaac Bautista created it as such from stars near the south celestial pole in the late 16th century. It appears near the Chameleon, and there represents his prey. When Plancius published his celestial globe around 1597, he changed it to a fly, and so it has remained ever since. The Engraved Hourglass Nebula (MyCn 18) is located within Musca, some 8,000 light years from Sol. It is a planetary nebula that was discovered by Annie Jump Cannon and Margaret Walton Mayall at Harvard College in the early 20th century, but limitations in instrumentation kept its characteristic shape hidden until 1996. The resolving power of the Hubble Space Telescope allowed it to produce an image revealing the nebula's shape as that of two epiconcentric rings with an eye-like structure at their focus. The nature and origins of this "eye" are not currently well understood.

NORMA,
the Carpenter's Square

Genitive	Abbr.	Prod. Adj.	Ind. Adj.
Normae	Nor	Normid	Normean

The French astronomer Lacaille created this constellation from his observations of the southern sky in the 1750s. It represents a carpenter's square, which was an important tool in ship-building during the Age of Exploration. A fascinating object known as Abell 3627 exists within Norma. It is a galaxy cluster of tremendous mass about 200 million light years distant. Because of its high mass, some have theorized it to be the Great Attractor, whose gravity is pulling the Local Group, the Hydra-Centaurus Supercluster and the Virgo Supercluster towards it at relative speeds estimated to be between 600-1,000 kilometers per second. [Wilkins & Dunn]

OCTANS,
the Octant

Genitive	Abbr.	Prod. Adj.	Ind. Adj.
Octantis	Oct	Octantid	Octantian

The Octant is a very faint constellation, but it is special because it contains the south celestial pole. The star σ Octantis is close enough to the pole to be considered a southern pole star, but it is too dim to be useful for navigation at magnitude +5.45. Lacaille invented the star figure on his star charts in 1756, and he named it for the octant, a navigational instrument similar to a sextant, but utilizing an arc of only 45°, a mere eighth of a circle.

OPHIUCHUS,
the Serpent Bearer

Genitive	Abbr.	Prod. Adj.	Ind. Adj.
Ophiuchi	Oph	Ophiuchid	Ophiuchian

Ὀφιοῦχος *(Ophiuchus)* is seen grasping a great serpent as he straddles the ecliptic. His name literally means "serpent-bearer" in Greek. In ancient Hellas, they imagined him as the healer god Ἀσκληπιός *(Asclepius)*. Asclepius was not always immortal. He discovered the secrets of medicine when he walked the earth and one day observed a serpent bringing healing herbs to another. Asclepius became so successful at keeping death at bay that Hades complained to Zeus that fewer souls were coming to the underworld, and so asked Zeus to eliminate Asclepius. Zeus complied with his brother's request and struck the healer dead by a thunderbolt. Later feeling remorse, Zeus resurrected Asclepius as a god and placed his mortal remains among the stars. The snake-entwined Rod of Asclepius is still the symbol of medicine today.

ORION,
the Hunter

Genitive	Abbr.	Prod. Adj.	Ind. Adj.
Orionis	Ori	Orionid	Orionian

Orion is, perhaps, the most well-known constellation in the sky. Most cultures around the globe have at least one story relating to the stars of Orion. The Babylonians called him MUL.SIPA.ZI.AN.NA, "the Heavenly Shepherd," or "True Shepherd of Anu." Anu was the chief god of the sky realm and lord of the constellations. It was believed that the stars owed their existence to Anu, and that he had created them as soldiers, whose charge was to seek out and destroy the wicked. The Anu cult centered around the Eanna Temple, on the banks of the Euphrates at Uruk, the ancient capital of the legendary king Gilgamesh. Gilgamesh was a demigod, possessing superhuman strength, and he is said to have built the walls of Uruk himself. In Earth's oldest story, Gilgamesh rules justly, but, after securing the city from external threats, he becomes restless and begins to go mad with rage. The people cry out for the gods to save them from the king's madness. The goddess Aruru sends Enkidu, a wild man, from the wilderness into the city of Uruk. There, he finds the warrior king, Gilgamesh. The two wrestle. Being equals in strength, they wrestle for a long time, but Gilgamesh eventually prevails. They became great friends and constant companions through many adventures. In one escapade, Enkidu is killed by Gugalanna, the Great Bull of Heaven, and Gilgamesh is devastated. He then went on a quest for immortality, which he may have found, as oft was he associated with the stars of Orion that we see even today.

PAVO,

the Peacock

Genitive	Abbr.	Prod. Adj.	Ind. Adj.
Pavonis	Pav	Pavonid	Pavonian

Pavo was created by Plancius in 1597. The peacock was sacred to Hera, whose servant was Ἄργος Πανόπτης *(Argos Panoptes)*, meaning "Argus the All-seeing." Hera set Argus on the task of guarding Ἰώ *(Io)*, the nymph who was changed into a heifer and chained to a sacred olive tree to keep her away from Zeus, who meant to breed her to create a new order upon Olympus. To free Io, Zeus sent Hermes, who charmed Argus, putting all of his eyes to sleep and slaying him with a stone's throw to the head. Hera commemorated her slain servant in the visage of her sacred bird, the peacock, whose tail feathers sport bright blue spots reminiscent of the eyes of Argus.

PEGASUS,
the Winged Horse

Genitive	Abbr.	Prod. Adj.	Ind. Adj.
Pegasi	Peg	Pegasid	Pegasusian

Πήγασος *(Pegasus)* was born of Medusa's blood falling into the sea when Perseus removed her head. He had only one rider, the hero Βελλεροφῶν *(Bellerophon)*, who was able to mount Pegasus when he stopped to drink near a fountain atop Ἑλικών *(Mt. Helicon)*. Bellerophon rode Pegasus into battle with the Χίμαιρα *(Chimæra)*. After the two emerged victorious, Zeus placed the winged steed into the sky.

PERSEUS,
the Hero

Genitive	Abbr.	Prod. Adj.	Ind. Adj.
Persei	Per	Perseid	Persian

This old constellation was in Ptolemy's *Almagest*. It represents Περσεύς *(Perseus)*, the hero who slew Μέδουσα *(Medusa)* and rescued Andromeda. Perseus is said to have been the legendary founder of Persia, the kingdom that bears his name. Perseus was born to Δανάη *(Danaë)* daughter of Ἀκρίσιος *(Acrisius)* of Ἄργος *(Argos)*. Acrisius had no male heirs, and, worrying about this, he visited an oracle to see what he could do about it. The oracle said that he would have none, but that Danaë would have a son, who would be destined to be Arcisius' doom. To prevent such a fate, Acrisius locked his daughter up in a bronze tower, forever keeping her from potential suitors. Zeus, seeing her predicament, pitied her and visited her as a shower of golden rain. Zeus' touch stirred her fertile womb, and Perseus was born. Years later, long after his run-in with Medusa, Perseus went to Λάρισα *(Larissa)* to compete in the games there. As the fates would have it, Acrisius was in the audience that day, but he chose the worst seat in the place. One of Perseus' javelin throws went awry, flying into the stands and piercing the aged kings heart, thus fulfilling the prophecy.

PHOENIX,
the Phoenix

Genitive	Abbr.	Prod. Adj.	Ind. Adj.
Phoenicis	Phe	Phoenicid	Phoenicean

Petrus Plancius first included the Phoenix on his small celestial globe published in about 1597. The φοῖνιξ (Phoenix) is a well known Greek character, being a great bird of extremely long life, but when it died it burst into flames and the new Phoenix rose from its ashes. It was closely associated with the sun, which was born in the east, passed through the sky, died in the west, and was reborn in the east with each new day. It was also a symbol of early Christianity and the empowerment of life after death.

PICTOR,
the Painter's Easel

Genitive	Abbr.	Prod. Adj.	Ind. Adj.
Pictoris	Pic	Pictorid	Pictorian

Lacaille created this faint southern constellation in 1756. He originally called it *le Chevalet et la Palette*, "the easel and palette" in French. As previously mentioned, it is quite a dim constellation, with its brightest star being magnitude +3.3. It is noteworthy for being the home region of RR Pictoris, a nova that flared to magnitude +1.2 in 1925. Included here also is Kapteyn's Star, a red dwarf, some 12.78 light years distant that exhibits the largest proper motion of any star after Barnard's Star. Peculiarly, Kapteyn's Star moves about the Milky Way in a way contrary to most stars, leading astronomers to believe that it was once part of a dwarf galaxy that merged with ours long ago. [Kaler 2002]

PISCES,
the Fishes

Genitive	Abbr.	Prod. Adj.	Ind. Adj.
Piscium	Pis	Piscid	Piscean

Cuneiform tablets from the first millennium B.C. refer to a constellation known as DU.NU.NU, which means "the fish cord." The Greeks told a tale of Ἀφροδίτη *(Aphrodite)* and Ἔρως *(Eros)* changing themselves into fish to escape the clutches of Τυφῶν

(Typhon), the most horrible of all Greek monsters. The two fishes were said to have tied themselves together to keep from losing one another.

PISCIS AUSTRINUS,
the Southern Fish

Genitive	Abbr.	Prod. Adj.	Ind. Adj.
Piscis Austrini	PsA	Piscis Austrinid	Piscis Austrinian

The Southern Fish is a very old constellation that was first recorded by the Ancient Babylonians as MUL.KU, "the fish." It was on Ptolemy's list, and, up until the 20th century, it was also known as Piscis Notius, meaning "well-known fish" or "famous fish" in Latin. Its stars are all quite dim, save one: first magnitude Fomalhaut, 18th brightest in the whole sky. It is a main-sequence star some 25 light years distant, and it is surrounded by a circumstellar disk. It is also the parent star of the first planet directly imaged at visible wavelengths, Fomalhaut b. [Kalas]

PUPPIS,
the Stern

Genitive	Abbr.	Prod. Adj.	Ind. Adj.
Puppis	Pup	Puppid	Puppian

Puppis is Latin for "poop deck," and the constellation represents the stern of Argo Navis, the Ship of the Argonauts. The Ship was once a single, large constellation, but in 1756, the Frenchman Lacaille divided it into three pieces: Puppis (the stern), Carina (the keel) and Vela (the sails). Puppis is a region of great interest in exoplanet research, as many extrasolar worlds have been found there.

PYXIS,
the (Mariner's) Compass

Genitive	Abbr.	Prod. Adj.	Ind. Adj.
Pyxidis	Pyx	Pyxid	Pyxidian

Lacaille created this constellation, too, and he called it Pyxis Nautica, the Naval or Mariner's Compass. Today, we shorten the name to just *Pyxis*. The Pyxidian region is home to T Pyxidis, a recurrent nova that erupted in 1890, 1902, 1920, 1944, 1966 and 2011. T Pyxidis is a binary made up of a sun-like star and a white dwarf located 15,600 light years from Earth. There is evidence that the mass of the white dwarf component of T Pyxidis is near the Chandrasekhar limit. If it were to continue to draw mass from its sun-like companion, it would collapse under its own weight, a tremendous calamity that would result in the brilliant display we known as a Type 1a supernova. [Schaefer, et. al]

RETICULUM,
the Reticle

Genitive	Abbr.	Prod. Adj.	Ind. Adj.
Reticuli	Ret	Reticulid	Reticulian

Reticulum is a faint constellation of the southern sky. Like many constellations in this region, it was created by Lacaille after his observations of the southern sky at the Cape of Good Hope in the 1750s. He named it for the reticle of his telescope finder. The star ζ Reticuli is of note, as it is supposedly the home of the alien abductors of Betty and Barney Hill of Portsmouth, New Hampshire. The Hills were out one late summer night in 1961, when a UFO was said to have appeared in the sky as they were driving back to New Hampshire from Niagara Falls in their 1957 Chevrolet Bel Air. The craft was reported to have followed them as they drove across the countryside that night, eventually absconding with the Hills and their car, only to return them the next day, dazed, and with broken wristwatches. [Fuller] The site of the UFO's first close approach to the Hills is marked by a state historical marker. [Jordan]

SAGITTA,
the Arrow

Genitive	Abbr.	Prod. Adj.	Ind. Adj.
Sagittae	Sge	Sagittid	Sagittean

Its name means "arrow" in Latin, and it is among the smallest constellations of the northern sky. It lies amongst the boundaries of the well-known Summer Triangle asterism. Sagitta is quite faint, having no stars brighter than magnitude +3, but is has a distinctive shape that can be recognized quite readily. Many cultures associated it with an arrow, including the Greeks, Persians, and Romans. *As-Sahm* was its name in Arabic, and today its brightest star retains the second part of that ancient moniker.

SAGITTARIUS,
the Archer

Genitive	Abbr.	Prod. Adj.	Ind. Adj.
Sagittarii	Sgr	Sagittariid	Sagittarian

The centaur archer is another ancient constellation that appeared in Ptolemy's *Almagest*. It existed long before the A.D. second century, though. The Babylonians saw him as Nergal, a bizarre creature similar to a centaur, but with the body of a lion instead of a horse. Images of Nergal famously adorned the Nergal Gate of Nineveh, in modern-day Iraq. The son of Enlil and Ninlil, Nergal presided over the underworld and was head of government in the affairs of the dead. One of his many attributes was that of fire and passions of war, and so he was often associated with the planet Mars. Given that he displayed these attributes, and that he was part of a pantheon that rivaled Judaism and Christianity, it should come as no surprise that Nergal often found himself depicted as being demonic, even as being Satan himself.

SCORPIUS,
the Scorpion

Genitive	Abbr.	Prod. Adj.	Ind. Adj.
Scorpii	Sco	Scorpiid	Scorpionic

Scorpius is a large constellation of the southern sky, located near the core of the Milky Way as viewed from Earth. The Babylonians called him MUL.GIR.TAB, which literally means "the creature with a burning sting." His claws were also referenced as "the Scales" in the MUL.APIN, a set of cuneiform sky tablets. Greek tales about Scorpius almost always feature Orion, whom he fatally stings in battle, and in whose name Sagittarius seeks revenge. Their constellations are placed well in the sky for the retelling of this story, as they are opposite one another, and when one is rising, the other is setting. This concept of cyclical birth, death, and rebirth finds its way into Christian tradition in the idea of the resurrection of Christ and of the rebirth of men made possible by the Lamb's sacrifice. In the story of Orion and the Scorpion, Orion was a great hunter who boasted to Artemis, goddess of the hunt, that he could kill every animal on Earth. Offended, Artemis sent Scorpius to deal with the hunter and to teach him a lesson he would not soon forget. The battle was fierce and it endured for a long time, eventually catching the attention of Zeus. Scorpius killed Orion in that battle, and Zeus placed them both into the sky to serve as a reminder to men about the dangers of pride. And so, the tale is told and retold each year. In autumn, Orion rises in the east, boasting of his skill, and then passes away in the west each spring, making way for the Scorpion to have his days in the summer. Scorpius, too will pass away, falling to Sagittarius' arrow, passing away in the west before Orion is reborn in the east and the whole tale repeats, as it has for millennia.

SCULPTOR,
the Sculptor

Genitive	Abbr.	Prod. Adj.	Ind. Adj.
Sculptoris	Scl	Sculptorid	Sculptorian

Lacaille named Sculptor in 1756, originally calling it *Apparatus Sculptoris*, the Sculptor's Studio. It is a fitting name, as there are many faint stars scattered throughout the region that could be imagined as bits of stone flecked away from some masterwork in progress. One of its notable denizens is the Cartwheel Galaxy, which is a compound lenticular and ring galaxy that is believed to have been produced as the result of a collision between a spiral with a smaller companion. [Amran]

SCUTUM,
the Shield

Genitive	Abbr.	Prod. Adj.	Ind. Adj.
Scuti	Sct	Scutid	Scutian

Scutum is unique among the constellations in that it is the only one whose iconography is not classical. It represents the Shield of Sobieski, King of Poland and Grand Duke of Lithuania, who reigned from 1674 until his death in 1696. His shield was placed into the sky by Hevelius in 1684 to commemorate Sobieski's victory in the Battle of Vienna a year earlier. Scutum is home to the Wild Duck Cluster (M11), whose brighter stars may remind the observer of a flock of ducks taking wing through the eyepiece.

SERPENS,
the Serpent

Genitive	Abbr.	Prod. Adj.	Ind. Adj.
Serpentis	Ser	Serpentid	Serpentian

Serpens is unique in that it is the only constellation that is discontiguous, being bifurcated by Ophiuchus, the Serpent Bearer, who is seen as grasping and holding the serpent behind his back. The two portions of the serpent are known as Serpens Caput (Serpent's Head) and Serpens Cauda (Serpent's Tail). Its brightest star is known by the traditional name *Unukalhai*, which means "the serpent's neck." Some star charts list this star as *Cor Serpentis* (Latin, "Serpent's Heart"). Hoag's Object is a perfectly proportioned face-on ring galaxy located in Serpens Caput. Another ring galaxy can be seen in the distance through the gap between the core and ring of Hoag's Object. The mechanics behind ring galaxy formation are not currently known. Noah Brosch hypothesizes that conditions may have arisen within these galaxies that led to instability in the bar structure of barred spirals that leads to that region going dark, leaving only the luminous core and a ring of active star formation regions. [Brosch]

SEXTANS,
the Sextant

Genitive	Abbr.	Prod. Adj.	Ind. Adj.
Sextantis	Sex	Sextantid	Sextantian

Sextans is a small constellation that lies on the celestial equator. It was created by Hevelius in 1687 to represent a sextant. He imagined the sky sextant as an astronomical instrument that derives its name for the Latin term for one-sixth of a circle (an arc of 60°). Sextants were used to measure the angular distance between stars, and they were the prime technology employed by astronomers in the pre-telescopic age.

TAURUS,
the Bull

Genitive	Abbr.	Prod. Adj.	Ind. Adj.
Tauri	Tau	Taurid	Taurian

Taurus might be the oldest of all the constellations. Michael Rappenglück of the University of Munich posits that a painting in the Hall of the Bulls in the caves at Lascaux, France depicts the constellation, complete with the Pleiades star cluster. [Rappenglück] The Lascaux paintings date to about 15,000 B.C., during the Paleolithic Era, or Old Stone Age. They represent not a bull in our modern experience, but an aurochs, a great wild Eurasian bovine that has been extinct since 1627. The Babylonians knew Taurus as Gugalanna, the Great Bull of Heaven, and he was listed in the MUL.APIN as

GU.GU.AN.NA. In the Epic of Gilgamesh, the goddess Ishtar sends Gugalanna to confront Gilgamesh in retribution for his spurning of her sexual advances. The constellation Orion sometimes represented Gilgamesh, and we see him in battle with the Bull in the night sky.

TELESCOPIUM,
the Telescope

Genitive	Abbr.	Prod. Adj.	Ind. Adj.
Telescopii	Tel	Telescopid	Telescopian

The French astronomer Lacaille created this constellation in 1756 to commemorate the advances made possible in astronomy by the invention of the telescope. Interestingly, Ptolemy included its brightest star, α Telescopii, in Corona Australis.

TRIANGULUM,
the Triangle

Genitive	Abbr.	Prod. Adj.	Ind. Adj.
Trianguli	Tri	Triangulid	Triangulian

Triangulum is a small constellation of the northern sky that lies between Andromeda and Aries. Triangulum and γ Andromedae made the constellation known to the Babylonians as MUL.APIN (the Plow). MUL.APIN is the first constellation listed on a set of cuneiform clay tablets that served as a compendium of sky features, and scholars today refer to that important work by its incipit.

TRIANGULUM AUSTRALE,
the Southern Triangle

Genitive	Abbr.	Prod. Adj.	Ind. Adj.
Trianguli Australis	TrA	Trianguli Australid	Trianguli Australean

Originally called Triangulus Antarticus, Petrus Plancius added this constellation as part of his celestial globe around 1597. Bayer gave it its current name in his *Uranumetria* in 1603. It was further refined in 1756 by Lacaille, when he included it, alongside Norma and Circinus, as part of a set of draftsman's instruments.

TUCANA,
the Toucan

Genitive	Abbr.	Prod. Adj.	Ind. Adj.
Tucanae	Tuc	Tucanid	Tucanean

Plancius created this southern constellation, as well. It represents the long-beaked tropical toucan. 47 Tucanae is a globular cluster within Tucana, located a little over 16,300 light years from Earth. It is the home of several blue stragglers, which are oddities among globular denizens in that they are young and hot. It is thought that they form when two stars merge within the cluster, forming more energetic progeny. [Leonard]

Ursa Major, the Greater Bear

Ursa Minor, the Lesser Bear

Genitive	Abbr.	Prod. Adj.	Ind. Adj.
Ursae Majoris	UMa	Ursae Majorid	Ursae Majorian
Ursae Minoris	UMi	Ursae Minorid	Ursae Minorian

Ursa Major is the famous home of the Big Dipper asterism. The seven bright stars of the Big Dipper are known to the Hindus as *Saptarishi*, the seven sages. Egyptians imagined it as the severed limb of Seth, torn from his body in a battle with Horus. Resolving the optical double of Mizar and Alcor, located at the bend in the Dipper's handle, was the vision test of the Roman army. The Greeks told the tale of Καλλιστώ (Callisto), one of the nymphs of Artemis, after whom Zeus lusted powerfully. Callisto would only be with Artemis, so Zeus disguised himself as such and seduced her. Born of this union was Ἀρκάς (Arcas), who was destined to become ruler of the people who would become known as the Arcadians. Hera, Zeus' wife, was furious and changed Callisto into a bear, whereupon she fled into the wilderness. Years later, Arcas was out hunting when he encountered a bear in the woods. It was Callisto, and when she saw her son, she ran to embrace him. Arcas, not knowing it was his mother, knocked an arrow in his bow and was about to shoot when - ZA-BLAM! - Zeus hurled a thunderbolt and, in a flash, changed Arcas into a bear, too. He then reunited mother and son in the sky, so that they could be together forever. Today, we see them as the constellations Ursa Major (Callisto) and Ursa Minor (Arcas).

VELA,
the Sails

Genitive	Abbr.	Prod. Adj.	Ind. Adj.
Velorum	Vel	Velorid	Velorean

Vela was created by Lacaille when he split up the ancient constellation Argo Navis, the Ship of the Argonauts, of which Vela makes up the sails. The False Cross is an asterism found in this region. It is a cruciform shape made up of the stars δ and κ Velorum and ι and ε Carinae that can be easily confused with Crux, the Southern Cross, a mistake that could wreak havoc in astronavigation.

VIRGO,
the Virgin

Genitive	Abbr.	Prod. Adj.	Ind. Adj.
Virginis	Vir	Virginid	Virginian

The MUL.APIN references this constellation as MUL.AB.SIN, the "seed furrow." It represented Shala, Sumerian goddess of grain, and her ear of barley. *Spica*, the constellation's brightest star, means "ear of grain" in Latin. The Romans associated Virgo with Ceres, goddess of grain, and from whose name we get the word *cereal*. It was the grace of Ceres that allowed humans to discover spelt, the yoking of oxen and the planting of fields, and it was through this grace that humans were able to settle down and establish law and order. Virgo rises early each northern summer in our time, right at the time of harvest for winter wheat.

VOLANS,
the Flying Fish

Genitive	Abbr.	Prod. Adj.	Ind. Adj.
Volantis	Vol	Volantid	Volantian

Piscis Volans was this constellation's original name when it was created by Petrus Plancius in around 1597. The Lindsay-Shapley Ring, a combination ring and lenticular galaxy, somewhat like the Cartwheel Galaxy, is a notable object that lies within this constellation's borders.

VULPECULA,
the Little Fox

Genitive	Abbr.	Prod. Adj.	Ind. Adj.
Vulpeculae	Vul	Vulpeculid	Vulpeculean

Smack-dab in the middle of the Summer Triangle, Vulpecula was created by Hevelius in the 17th century. He called it *Vulpecula cum ansere*, meaning "the little fox with the goose," in Latin. Today, the goose remains only in the proper name *Anser*, which is ascribed to the star α Vulpeculae.

Chapter V:

ADJECTIVALS

of

GENERAL BODIES

Name	Adjective
asteroid	asteroidal
comet	cometary
cosmos	cosmic
ecliptic	ecliptical zodiacal
equinox	equinoctial
galaxy	galactic
meteor	meteoric
meteorite	meteoritic
meteoroid	meteoroidal
nebula	nebular
planet	planetary
planetoid	planetoidal
quasar	quasaric
sky	celestial
solstice	solsticial
star	stellar astral sidereal
supernova	supernovan
universe	universal

Appendix A:

GREEK LETTERS

This book makes frequent use of Ancient Greek in the form of names for places, people and characters from Greek history and myth. This practice is not done to look fancy, but to add authenticity. Many Ancient Greek terms have no direct English equivalent, and any Greek person would, after all, sign their name using the Greek alphabet, not the Latin one. For these reasons, Ancient Greek words are used in this book when they are first introduced. They are then followed by Latin versions and/or English equivalents in parentheses. All subsequent uses are either Latin or English for the sake of positive flow. To allow those interested to decipher and to pronounce properly the Ancient Greek used in this book, the following introduction to Greek letters and pronunciation is provided. Phonetics discussed and described herein are for Ancient Greek (not Modern Greek, unless so noted), and they are referenced from the *Handbook of the International Phonetic Association: A guide to the use of the International Phonetic Alphabet*, International Phonetic Association, Cambridge University Press, 1999.

Identifying Greek Letters

Often, modern folk are not accustomed to Hellenic script. The Ελληνικό αλφάβητο *(Helleniko Alphabeto)*, or the Greek alphabet, is composed of 24 unique letters, ordered from alpha to omega. The term *alphabet* comes from the first two Greek letters, **alpha** and **bet**a. Having been in use since around the 8th century B.C., the Greek alphabet descended from the earlier Phoenician alphabet, a type of consonant only alphabet known as an *abjad*. Abjads left it up to the speaker to supply the appropriate vowel sounds.

In astronomy, Greek letters are notably used in Bayer designation of stars. First produced by Johann Bayer in 1603, his catalog, *Uranometria*, identified specific stars by a Greek letter, followed by the genitive form of the constellation in which the star appeared. Usually, the brightest star in the constellation received the designation of α (alpha), which is the first letter of the Greek alphabet, followed in order thereafter (see chart below).

Despite this general scheme, Bayer did not always adhere to it, meaning that α is not always the brightest star in a given constellation. In Bayer's day, there was no precise method by which to measure stellar brightness. Stars were traditionally grouped into six magnitude (brightness) classes. Bayer's catalog lists all the first magnitude stars, followed by all the second, and so forth; he made no effort to arrange stars according to magnitude within each of the six classes. Sometimes, he arranged stars according to their arrangement within a constellation, and other times it was his own arbitrary choice. With Bayer being gone, we will perhaps never know the intricacies of his thought process.

On the next page is a table with each letter of the Hellenic Alphabet in order with names and phonetics. Some letter names are pronounced differently between Ancient and Modern Greek. For those letters, the Ancient pronunciation is designated *(anc.)* and the Modern pronunciation is designated *(mod.)*.

Letter	Name	Letter	Name
α	alpha (AL-fuh)	ν	nu (NYOO)
β	beta (BAY-tuh)	ξ	xi (KSEE)
γ	gamma (GAHM-uh)	ο	omicron (OH-me-kron)
δ	delta (DEL-tuh)	π	pi (anc. PEE; mod. PIE)
ε	epsilon (EPP-see-lon)	ρ	rho (RO)
ζ	zeta (ZAY-tuh)	σ*	sigma (SIG-muh)
η	eta (AY-tuh)	τ	tau (rhymes with "now")
θ	theta (THAY-tuh)	υ	upsilon (OOP-see-lon)
ι	iota (eye-OH-tuh)	φ	phi (anc. FEE; mod. FYE)
κ	kappa (KAP-uh)	χ	chi (KYE)
λ	lambda (LAM-duh)	ψ	psi (anc. PSEE; mod. SYE)
μ	mu (MYOO)	ω	omega OH-me-guh)

*There are two versions of lower-case sigma: normal (σ) and final (ς). The normal character should always be used in Bayer designation, as the final character is only used when it is the final character in a Greek word.

Pronouncing Greek Letters

This section discusses the sounds represented by each of the Greek letters and how they are transliterated into English. The spelling of each letter in both Greek and English is presented, as well as information about diacritics, or accent marks, often used in Ancient Greek.

Aα - ἄλφα (alpha)

Alpha is the first letter of the Greek alphabet. It is transliterated into English as *Aa*. Its sound is /a/ as in *father*. There are long and short versions of alpha's sound, but, unlike in English, the difference between them is simply how long the sound is held. For example, short alpha is /a/, as in the initial sound of *away*, while long alpha is /a/ as in *father*.

The diacritics (˝) used in the spelling of *ἄλφα* convey two important details about how the initial sound of the word is to be made. The mark on the left (ʼ) is called the *ψιλὸν πνεῦμα (psilòn pneûma)* in Ancient Greek, or *psili* in Modern Greek. It indicates that a sound be made with smooth breathing at the beginning of a word, or without the **voiceless glottal fricative** /h/, as in *high*. The second mark is the *ὀξεῖα (oxeîa)*, called *oxia* in modern times, which means "sharp," or "high." It indicates high pitch on a short vowel and rising pitch on a long vowel. In the case of *ἄλφα*, the initial *α* is long, and the oxia represents rising pitch. Both the long and short versions of alpha's sound are known as the **open front unrounded vowel** in phonetics.

Ββ - βῆτα (beta)

Beta is the second letter of the Greek alphabet. It is transliterated into English as *Bb*. Its sound in Ancient Greek is /b/, as in *boy*. This sound is called a **voiced labial plosive**. In Modern Greek, its sound is /v/, as in *velvet*, a **voiced labiodental fricative**.

The diacritic that appears over the eta in *βῆτα* is a circumflex, or περισπωμένη *(perispōménē)*, as it is called in Ancient Greek. This mark takes many forms; see the ἦτα *(eta)* entry for more information on circumflexes in Ancient Greek.

Γγ - γάμμα (gamma)

The third letter of the Greek alphabet is gamma. It is transliterated into English as *Gg*. Gamma represents the sound /g/ as in *goose*. Phoneticists call this sound a **plain g**, or a **voiced velar stop**.

Δδ - δέλτα (delta)

Delta is the fourth letter of the Greek alphabet. It is transliterated into English as *Dd*, and it represents the **voiced dental plosive** sound /d/, as in *dog*.

Εε - ἔψιλόν (epsilon)

Epsilon is the fifth letter of the Greek alphabet. It is transliterated into English as *Ee*. Its sound is short /e/ as in *egg*: a **close-mid front unrounded vowel** sound. It is sometimes written with the psili to avoid confusion with the sound represented by the seventh Greek letter ἦτα (eta), which is discussed later in this text.

The diacritics over the epsilon in *ἔψιλόν* are the psili (as with ἄλφα) and *βαρεῖα (bareîa)*, or *baria*, which means "heavy," or "low."   It tells the speaker to pronounce the sound with normal or low pitch.

Zζ - ζῆτα (zeta)

Zeta is the sixth letter of the Greek alphabet. It is transliterated into English as *Zz*. The sound value it had in antiquity is a matter of dispute.   Some scholars believe it to have had a sound /zd/ as in *Mazda*, a **voiced alveolar fricative** sound, while others believe it was /dz/ as in *adze,* a **voiced alveolar affricate**. There are strong arguments for either pronunciation, and the differences between them could have been a matter of dialect.

Ηη - ἤτα (eta)

Eta is the seventh Greek letter.   Its English transliteration is *Ēē*.   Originally, the letter had the consonant value /h/ as in *Hippocrates*. This sound led to the development of the Latin letter Hh, which represents the **voiceless glottal fricative** sound /h/ as in *heat.* That heritage is reflected by the similarity of the Greek and Latin glyphs, including in the lower case, where *η* represents a half *H*.   Sometime in the fifth century B.C., the /h/ sound of eta disappeared throughout Hellas. It was replaced with a mild range of sounds that varied by dialect. In the East Ionic dialect, eta came to be pronounced as the **open-mid front unrounded vowel** /aː/ or /ɛ/ as in English *bed*.   In Attica, it represented the **close-mid front unrounded vowel sound** and it was pronounced as the diphthong /eɪ/ as in *eight*.

The accent used above eta in its spelling (᾿) is a combination of the ψιλὸν πνεῦμα (psilòn pneûma), or psili, with the περισπωμένη (perispōménē), or perispomeni. As previously discussed, the psili (') represents smooth breathing. (See ἄλφα above.) Περισπωμένη (perispōménē) means "twisted around" in Ancient Greek. In Modern Greek, it is perispomeni. The perispomeni (^) is equivalent to a circumflex, which indicates long vowels with high and then falling pitch. Circumflexes may be rendered in many ways, from peaks to simple curves to wavy lines, but they are always above the character. Different fonts render differently, so the perispomeni, or circumflex, may look different from one place to another, depending upon the font used.

Θθ - θῆτα (theta)

Theta is the eighth letter of the Greek alphabet. A mnemonic to help you remember the order of Greek letters is "zeta ate a theta." It is transliterated into English as the digraph *th*, which is pronounced /θ/ as in *thermometer*, a **voiceless dental fricative**. Note the phonetic symbol used is theta itself. A bit of circular logic now and again never hurt anyone, says I: which brings us to the next letter...

Ιι - ἰῶτα (iota)

Among the Greek letters, iota is ninth in order. Its English transliteration is *Ii*. The phrase, "Not one iota," meaning "not the least bit," comes from the Greek letter iota, especially its lower case, which is simply a vertical stroke with a tiny bit of baseline serif: the most basic of writing elements. The term *jot*, meaning "the least bit" or "to write hastily" descends directly from *iota*. In Ancient Greek, there are both long and short sounds for iota. The short sound is pronounced as the **near-close** near-front unrounded vowel /ɪ/ as in *pit*. By contrast, the long sound is pronounced as the close front unrounded vowel /iː/ as in *free*.

Κκ - κάππα (kappa)

Kappa is the tenth Greek letter. It is transliterated into English as *Kk*. Greek names for people and places using kappa are often transliterated with *Cc* because the ancient Romans transliterated them into contemporary Latin this way. Hence, Ἡρακλῆς *(Herakles)* is often written as *Heracles*, and so forth. Transliterations from Modern Greek always use *Kk*. Its sound is always the voiceless velar plosive /k/ as in *kangaroo*.

Λλ - λάμβδα (lambda)

The eleventh letter of the Greek alphabet is known in modern times as lambda, but there is some evidence that it was known classically as "labda." It is transliterated into English as *Ll*. As in English and Latin, lambda always has the /l/ sound, as in *letter*. In phonetics, this sound is called clear l, or the alveolar lateral approximant.

Μμ - μῦ (mu)

"Mu makes a dozen" is a mnemonic that can be helpful in remembering that mu is the twelfth Greek letter. Note the perispomeni (ˆ), or circumflex, over the upsilon (we will get to that letter soon enough) in the spelling *μῦ*; this diacritic tells us that the upsilon's sound is rounded, and that *μῦ* is not pronounced "moo," but "myoo." Mu is transliterated into English as *Mm*. Its sound is always /m/, as in *marmot*: a bilabial nasal consonantal sound.

Νν - νῦ (nu)

Nu is the thirteenth letter of the Greek alphabet. Its English transliteration is *Nn*. The perispomeni above the upsilon tells us that *νῦ* is pronounced "nyoo." Its sound is the **alveolar nasal** /n/, as in *nincompoop*.

Ξξ - ξεῖ (xi)

Xi is fourteenth in line, and one of the more unusual of Greek letters. The letter is pronounced /kʰséê/, and it is transliterated into English as *Xx*. It has the **consonantal cluster** sound /ks/, as in *ox*.

Οο - ὂ μικρόν (o mikron, omicron)

Letter number fifteen is omicron. Its name, *o mikron*, literally means "little o." It is transliterated into English as *Oo*. In Ancient Greek, it always has the **close-mid back rounded vowel** sound /o/, as in *obey*.

Ππ - πεῖ (pi)

The Ancient Greeks pronounced the sixteenth letter as /péê/. It is transliterated into English as *Pp*. Its sound is the **voiceless bilabial stop** /p/, as in *plethora*.

Ρρ - ῥῶ (rho)

Rho is the seventeenth Greek letter. The ancients pronounced it as "hro." It always represents a **trilled** or **flapped** /r/ sound, however, rho is a liquid consonant, meaning that its sound changes based upon its location in a word, much like a liquid's shape changes based upon the shape of its container. When rho initiates a word, it is pronounced with a rough breathing /h/ sound, as in *rhythm*. When rho appears within a word, its sound is trilled /r/, as in the Spanish *rr* in *perro*. Think "RRRuffles have rrridges."

It should also be noted that there are two variations of the lowercase rho, both of which may appear simultaneously on your device, albeit in different locations. Depending upon which font you have chosen, plain lowercase rho and lowercase rho with diacritics may render as two different variations of the glyph.

Σσς - σίγμα (sigma)

Sigma is the eighteenth letter in the Greek alphabet. It is unique in that it has three forms: uppercase (Σ), lowercase normal (σ), and lowercase final (ς). It is transliterated into English as *Ss*. Sigma's sound is the **voiceless alveolar fricative** /s/, as in *sassafras*.

Ττ - ταῦ (tau)

Tau is the nineteenth Greek letter. Its English transliteration is *Tt*, and it has a **voiceless alveolar stop** sound /t/, as in *telephone*.

Υυ - ὑψιλόν (upsilon)

The psili with perispomeni diacritic (᾿) dictates that the twentieth Greek letter is pronounced "OOP-see-lon." It is transliterated as *Yy* in English. In Ancient Greek, it represents /oo/, the **close back rounded vowel**, as it sounds in *loop*.

Φφ - φεῖ (phi)

The twenty-first letter of the Greek alphabet is phi. *Phi* is pronounced /ˈfiː/, as *fee*, and it is transliterated into English as the digraph *ph*. Phi represents the **aspirated voiceless bilabial plosive**, or /pʰ/ sound, in Ancient Greek: a sound that is quite similar to English *ph*, but with a slightly pronounced initial /p/ sound.

Χχ - χεῖ (chi)

Chi is the twenty-second Greek letter. Ancient Romans transliterated chi into Latin as the digraph *ch*, a practice that carries over into English. Unlike English *ch*, chi represents the **aspirated voiceless velar stop** /kʰ/. Thus, the Greek island Χίος is transliterated as *Chios*, and it is pronounced /ˈkhēˌäs/.

Ψψ - ψεῖ (psi)

Psi is the penultimate letter of the Greek alphabet: number 23. *Psi* is pronounced /ˈpsaɪ/ with a slight /p/ sound at the beginning. It is transliterated into English as the **consonantal cluster** *ps*, and it is pronounced /ps/ as in the final sound in *ellipse*.

Ωω - ὦ μέγα (omega)

The final letter of the Greek alphabet is the "Mega O," or the "Great O," thus *o-mega*. Like omicron, omega is transliterated into English as *Oo*, however, unlike omicron, omega is always a **long open-mid back rounded vowel** /o/, as made by *ough* in *thought* spoken in General American accent.

Exercise:

It is often helpful to practice writing the glyphs when attempting to learn them. Try writing them along with their English phonetics in repetition until you can readily recognize them. Making flash cards is helpful, as well. A practiced hand utilizing a slightly dulled pencil, fountain or dip pen produces aesthetically pleasing glyphs. Relax, breathe freely and have fun!

Appendix B:

CAPITALIZATION QUICK REFERENCE GUIDE

This quick reference guide may be used to efficiently find the correct word form for your astronomy writing. Words should be written as they appear here in the appropriate situations as indicated in parenthesis. Refer to Chapter 1 for more information.

Earth, Moon and Sun
Earth (when used as planet name)
earth (when preced. by *the* & referring to ground, soil or "the world.")
Moon (Earth's satellite)
moon (any other natural satellite; when used in phase names)
Sun (the star itself)
sun (the light in the sky)
Solar System

Equinoxes, Solstices and Cross-Quarters
Northward equinox
Southward equinox
March equinox
September equinox
vernal equinox
autumnal equinox
Northern solstice
Southern solstice
June solstice
December solstice
summer solstice
winter solstice
Lughnasadh [LOO-nuh-sah] (August 1)
Samhain [SAH-wehn] (November 1)
Imbolc [IM-olk or IM-olg] (February 1)
Beltaine (May 1)

Planets, Dwarf Planets
All are always capitalized

Exoplanet style

μ Arae d

Asteroid style

4581 Asclepius

Meteors and Meteorite falls

Cando Event

Chelyabinsk Meteor

Geminids

Star Names

Gemma

δ Pavonis

Supernovae

SN 1940B

Constellations

Piscis Austrinus, the Southern Fish

Deep Sky Objects

the Double Double

M6

NGC 1138

Andromeda Galaxy

Spacecraft & Rockets

Pioneer 10

Saturn V (roman numeral usually used when designation number less than 10)

Titan 34D

Bibliography

Allen, Richard Hinkley. *Star Names: Their Lore and Meaning.* Mineloa, New York: Dover, 1963.

Amram P, Mendes de Oliveira C, Boulesteix J, Balkowski C; Mendes De Oliveira; Boulesteix; Balkowski (February 1998). "The Hα kinematic of the Cartwheel galaxy". Astron Astrophys. 330: 881–93.

Apollodorus. *Mythographi Graeci ...: Fasc. I. Pseudo-Eratosthenis Catasterismi. Recensuit Alexander Olivieri. 1897. Fasc. Ii. Palaephati Peri Apiston. Heracliti ... Edidit Nicolaus (Latin Edition).* Charleston, South Carolina: Nabu Press, 2009.

Black, Jeremy. *Gods, Demons and Symbols of Ancient Mesopotamia: An Illustrated Dictionary.* Austin: University of Texas Press, 1992.

Bobrowsky, Matthew (1994), "Narrowband HST Imagery of the Young Planetary Nebula Henize 1357", The Astrophysical Journal 426: L47–L50.

Brandão, I. M. et al. (March 2011), "Asteroseismic modelling of the solar-type subgiant star β Hydri", Astronomy & Astrophysics 527: A37.

Brosch, N. (1985). "The nature of Hoag's object – The perfect ringed galaxy". Astronomy and Astrophysics 153 (1): 199–206.

Bulfinch, Thomas. *The Age of Fable.* New York: Grosset & Dunlap, 1913.

Condos, Theony. *Star Myths of the Greeks and Romans: A Sourcebook.* Newburyport, Massachusetts: Phanes Press, 1997.

Dalley, Stephanie. *Myths from Mesopotamia: Creation, the Flood, Gilgamesh, and Others.* New York: Oxford University Press USA, 2009.

Διονύσιος Ἀλεξάνδρου Ἁλικαρνᾶσσεύς, (Dionysios son of Aléxandros, of Halikarnassós). *Περὶ μιμήσεως, (Perì mimēseōs) On Imitation*, 41.

Fuller, John G. *Interrupted Journey*. New York: Berkley Publishing Group, 1975.

Hamilton, Edith. *Mythology: Timeless Tales of Gods and Heroes.* New York: Warner Books, 1969.

Herodotus., tr. by Aubrey de Selincourt. *Histories.* London: Penguin Classics, 1954.

Hesiod. *Theogeny.* London: Penguin Classics, 1976.

Houston, Walter Scott. "Deep Sky Wonders." Sky & Telescope. December 1980. Cambridge, Massachusetts: Sky Publishing, 1980.

Hyginus, Gaius Iulius. *Hygini Astronomica.* Paris: Librairie Honore Champion, 1909.

International Astronomical Union. "Naming of Astronomical Objects." Web. <http://www.iau.org/public/themes/naming/>. Retrieved 30 June 2012.

International Phonetic Association. (1999). Handbook of the International Phonetic Association: A guide to the use of the International Phonetic Alphabet. Cambridge: Cambridge University Press.

Jordan, Jessica (2011-07-25). "Little Green Men Celebrated in NH". NH.com. Retrieved 26 July 2013.

Kalas, Paul; et al. (2008). "Optical Images of an Exosolar Planet 25 Light-Years from Earth". Science 322 (5906): 1345–1348.

Kaler, James B. *The Hundred Greatest Stars*. New York: Copernicus Books, 2002. pp. 108–109.

Kaler, James B. *The Cambridge Encyclopedia of Stars*. Cambridge, England: Cambridge University Press, 2006.

King, Jeremy R. et al. (April 2003), "Stellar Kinematic Groups. II. A Reexamination of the Membership, Activity, and Age of the Ursa Major Group", The Astronomical Journal 125 (4): 1980–2017.

Leonard, Peter J. T. (1989). "Stellar collisions in globular clusters and the blue straggler problem". The Astronomical Journal 98: 217–226.

Lloyd, Lucy. "≠nabbe ta !nu (Corona Australis)." *The Digital Bleek & Lloyd*. University of Cape Town, 1873. <http://lloydbleekcollection.cs.uct.ac.za/stories/319/index.html>. Retrieved 16 August 2012.

Madore, Barry F. and Halton C. Arp, (1979). "Three new faint star clusters." Astrophysical Journal, Vol. 227, pp. L103-L104 and Plate L3-L6 [ADS: 1979ApJ...227L.103M]

Maiolino, R.; Krabbe, A.; Thatte, N.; Genzel, R. (1998). "Seyfert Activity and Nuclear Star Formation in the Circinus Galaxy". The Astrophysical Journal 493 (2): 650–65.

Mitchell, Steven. *Gilgamesh: A New English Version.* New York: Atria Books, 2006.

National Aeronautics and Space Administration (NASA). "NASA Spacecraft Embarks on Historic Journey Into Interstellar Space." <http://www.nasa.gov/mission_pages/voyager/voyager20130912.html#.UkPJniRgONJ>. Retrieved 26 September 2013.

Ovid., tr. by David Raeburn. *Metamorphoses.* London: Penguin Classics, 2004.

Pseudo-Apollodorus. *Bibliotheca.* London: Penguin Classics, 1974.

Rappenglück, Michael (2004). "A Paleolithic Planetarium Underground - The Cave of Lascaux (Part I)". Migration & Diffusion an International Journal.5 (18): 93-119.

Retter, A.; Zhang, B.; Siess, L.; Levinson, A. (May 22, 2006). "The planets capture model of V838 Monocerotis: conclusions for the penetration depth of the planet/s". Monthly Notices of the Royal Astronomical Society. 1 370 (3): 1565.

Ridpath, Ian; Tirion, Wil. *Stars and Planets Guide.* Princeton, New Jersey: Princeton University Press, 2001.

Schaefer, B.E.; Pagnotta, A.; Shara, M.; (2009). "The Nova Shell and Evolution of the Recurrent Nova T Pyxidis". Astrophys.J.708:381-402,2010.

Soker, N.; Tylenda, R. (June 15, 2006). "Modelling V838 Monocerotis as a Mergeburst Object". arXiv:astro-ph/0606371.

South African National Parks. "Table Mountain National Park - SAN Parks - Official Website, Main Attractions." <http://www.sanparks.org/parks/ table_mountain/tourism/attractions.php>. Retrieved 20 July 2013.

Squire, C. *The mythology of the British Islands: an introduction to Celtic myth, legend, poetry and romance*. London & Ware: UCL & Wordsworth Editions Ltd., 2000.

Staal, Julius D.W. *The New Patterns in the Sky*. Granville, Ohio: McDonald and Woodward Publishing Company, 1988.

Stahl, Jason. "20 Things You Didn't Know About... Aliens". Discover. Archived from the original on 21 February 2007. Retrieved 13 July 2013.

Stein, W A; O'Dell, S L; Strittmatter, P A (September 1976). "The BL Lacertae Objects". Annual Review of Astronomy and Astrophysics (Annual Reviews) 14: pp. 173–195.

Thompson, Gary D., tr. *MUL.APIN*. Web. <http:// members.westnet.com.au/Gary-David-Thompson/ page11-8.html>. Retrieved 20 March 2013.

Tylenda, R.; Soker, N.; Szczerba, R. (October 2005). "On the progenitor of V838 Monocerotis". Astronomy and Astrophysics 441 (3): 1099–1109.

White, Gavin. *Babylonian Star-lore. An Illustrated Guide to the Star-lore and Constellations of Ancient Babylonia.* Solaria Publications, 2008.

Wilkins, George A., ed. *IAU Style Manual: The Preparation of Astronomical Papers and Reports.* IAU, 1989. Web. <http://www.iau.org/static/publications/stylemanual1989.pdf>. Retrieved 15 October 2011.

Wilkins, Jamie; Dunn, Robert. *300 Astronomical Objects: A Visual Reference to the Universe.* Richmond Hill, Ontario: Firefly Books, 2006.

ABOUT THE AUTHOR

 Woodrow W. Grizzle III is a planetarian, science educator and Emmy® award-winning writer with more than a decade of experience in communicating the wonders of astronomy to the public. He is the Planetarium Director at Elizabeth City State University in Elizabeth City, North Carolina.

Woodrow's published works span many areas. He is an associate editor and regular contributor to *Southern Skies, the Journal of the Southeastern Planetarium Association* (SEPA), where his columns focus on the art of storytelling and archaeoastronomy, the study of ancient peoples' relationship with the sky. He regularly reviews books for *Planetarian, the Journal of the International Planetarium Society* (IPS). As part of his work in Elizabeth City, he writes science curricula for both formal and informal classroom settings.

Woodrow's work is guided by his passion for communicating the awe-inspiring field of astronomy through lively, immersive lectures, revealing demonstrations, and rich, compelling storytelling. His mantra is Relate, Reveal, Remember, reflecting his goals of relating the wonders of the universe to the populace, and revealing its majesty in a way that people will always remember.